123 Easy Pasta Sauce Recipes

(123 Easy Pasta Sauce Recipes - Volume 1)

Lucy Salinas

Content

123 Awesome Easy Pasta Sauce Recipes

***

---

1. Alla Checca Pasta Sauce Recipe

Serving: 4 | Prep: | Cook: 120mins |Ready in:

Ingredients

- 5 tomatoes, seeded and diced
- 4 cloves garlic, minced
- 1/2 cup chopped fresh basil
- 1 teaspoon chopped oregano
- 1/2 cup olive oil
- salt to taste
- 2 tablespoons grated parmesan cheese
- 1 pound pasta

Direction

- 1. Combine tomatoes, garlic, basil, oregano, and olive oil in a non-metal bowl. Stir in salt. Cover with plastic wrap. Allow to sit at room temperature at least 2 hours, or as long as 10 hours.
- 2. Cook pasta in a large pot of boiling salted water until al dente. Drain. Pour uncooked sauce over hot pasta, and toss. Add grated Parmesan cheese to your liking.

---

2. Alpha And Omega Pasta Sauce Recipe

Serving: 5 | Prep: | Cook: 120mins |Ready in:

Ingredients

- 6-7 cloves garlic
- Meat- .5-.6 lb ground beef, or 1 pkg of hot italian sausage
- 28 oz all purpose tomato sauce - I use Dei Fratelli
- 1 cup red table wine- Carlo Rossi for me
- 1/4-1/2 white onion
- basil
- rosemary
- oregano
- salt
- pepper
- extra virgin olive oil

Direction

- Mince garlic and chop onion
- Crumble and start to brown meat over medium heat
- In a large pot over medium heat, drizzle 2 tbsp. olive oil, then add garlic and onion.
- Wait until garlic is brown and onions are sweet.
- When meat is finished, drain on an old newspaper or paper towel.
- Add tomato sauce, meat, wine, and spices to taste (I do 1.5-2 tbsp. each) to pot with garlic and onions.
- Stir until it looks uniform.
- Simmer UNCOVERED for at least an hour, preferably 2 or more, stirring occasionally.
- And of course, make some pasta once you cannot wait any longer. I do either a penne or linguine, depending on the meat, mood, and moon phase.

---

3. Angel Hair Pasta With Creamy Mushroom Sauce Recipe

Serving: 4 | Prep: | Cook: 20mins |Ready in:

Ingredients

- 4 ounces angel hair pasta
- 1-1/2 cups sliced fresh mushrooms
- 1 medium white onion chopped
- 1 teaspoon butter
- 3 ounces cream cheese cut into cubes
- 1/4 teaspoon salt
- 1 teaspoon freshly ground black pepper
- 1-1/3 cups milk
- 2 tablespoons chives snipped

Direction

- Cook pasta according to package directions then drain well.
- In a medium saucepan cook the mushrooms and onion in the butter until vegetables are tender.
- Stir in cream cheese, salt and pepper then cook and stir over low heat until cheese is melted.
- Gradually stir in milk and chives and heat through.
- Pour sauce over pasta and toss to coat.
- Serve immediately.

4. Angel Hair Pasta With Fresh Tomato Sauce Recipe

Serving: 6 | Prep: | Cook: 20mins | Ready in:

Ingredients

- 1 small garlic clove
- 3 lb tomatoes
- 2 tablespoons fresh lemon juice
- 1 teaspoon salt
- 1 teaspoon sugar (optional)
- 1/2 teaspoon black pepper
- 1 lb dried capellini (angel-hair pasta)
- 1/2 cup chopped fresh basil
- ****
- Accompaniments:
- finely grated parmigiano-Reggiano
- extra-virgin olive oil for drizzling (optional)
- fresh Mozzarella broken into pieces (optional)

Direction

- Mince garlic and mash to a paste with a pinch of salt using a large heavy knife.
- Core and coarsely chop two thirds of tomatoes. Halve remaining tomatoes crosswise, then rub cut sides of tomatoes against large holes of a box grater set in a large bowl, reserving pulp and discarding skin. Toss pulp with chopped tomatoes, garlic paste, lemon juice, salt, sugar (if using), and pepper. Let stand until ready to use, at least 10 minutes.
- While tomatoes stand, cook pasta in a 6- to 8-quart pot of boiling salted water, uncovered, until al dente, about 2 minutes.
- Drain in a colander and immediately add to tomato mixture, tossing to combine. (Add fresh mozzarella at this point if you go that route).
- Sprinkle with basil.
- NOTE: Tomato mixture can stand at room temperature up to 2 hours.

5. Arugula Walnut Pesto Recipe

Serving: 46 | Prep: | Cook: 5mins | Ready in:

Ingredients

- These quantities are really just a starting a point. You may prefer more or less rosemary, etc. I just keep tasting as I go, adding more of this or that until I achieve a balanced flavour.
- 2 cups arugula leaves
- 1 clove garlic, chopped
- about 1/4 cup extra virgin olive oil (use the good stuff for this)
- about 1/4 cup walnuts
- about 2 tsp. fresh rosemary leaves
- salt and pepper to taste
- 1/4 small lemon

Direction

- Put the arugula leaves into your food processor and add 1 tsp. of rosemary, a small handful of the walnuts, and the garlic. Sprinkle all this with salt and grind over some pepper. Pour in a few tablespoons of olive oil and blend until smooth.
- Taste the pesto and then continue to add remaining rosemary, walnuts, additional salt and pepper, and olive oil, as you see fit. Be sure to add a little squirt of lemon at the very end--it helps retain the color and makes all the flavours a little brighter.

6. Asparagus Pesto Recipe

Serving: 6 | Prep: | Cook: 3mins | Ready in:

Ingredients

- 1 pound asparagus
- 1/2 cup chopped walnuts
- 1/4 cup grated Parmesan
- 1 shallot, chopped
- 1 clove garlic, minced
- salt to taste (optional)

Direction

- Bring a pot of salted water to boil and blanch asparagus for approximately three minutes. Drain water and chop asparagus into small pieces. Throw all ingredients into a blender (+ dash of salt) and blend until smooth.
- Use with your favorite pasta for a delicious meal!
- Note --I just used a bunch of asparagus and guessed it was about a pound. No shallots? I would recommend half of a small red onion as alternate. I chopped all the ingredients so they would fit comfortably in my blender but depending on your model you may not need to chop anything at all. Just throw it all in and blend!

7. Baked Whole Wheat Penne With Tomato Sauce Recipe

Serving: 6 | Prep: | Cook: 35mins | Ready in:

Ingredients

- 1 package whole wheat penne pasta
- 5 tomatoes grated
- 2 tablespoons tomato paste
- 1 small white onion chopped
- 2 cloves garlic sliced
- 2 red bell peppers chopped
- 1/2 cup black olives
- 1 teaspoon oregano leaves
- 1 teaspoon crushed pepper
- 1/2 teaspoon mint flakes
- 1/2 teaspoon black pepper
- 1/2 teaspoon ground cumin
- 1/4 teaspoon salt
- 1/4 bunch parsley chopped
- 1/4 cup olive oil
- 2 cups grated cheese
- 1 cup mushrooms
- 1 teaspoon fresh basil
- 1 cup fresh corn kernels

Direction

- Boil penne.
- In a deep skillet heat olive oil and stir in onions and garlic.
- Cook until onions are soft.
- Add peppers and olives then stir for 3 minutes then add the paste.
- Add mushrooms and stir for 3 minutes then add paste and stir 2 minutes longer.
- Stir in tomatoes, pepper, oregano, mint, cumin, salt, basil and corn.
- Simmer on low until tomatoes are cooked.
- After turning it off add parsley.
- In an oven dish put the penne, tomato sauce and 1/2 cup water.
- Mix well then cover with foil and bake in a preheated 375 oven for 25 minutes.

- After 25 minutes put the grated cheese on top and continue baking.

8. Basic Spaghetti Or Pasta Sauce Recipe

Serving: 8 | Prep: | Cook: 90mins |Ready in:

Ingredients

- 3 tbsp olive oil
- minced garlic or garlic powder to taste (I usually use at least 4 cloves)
- 12 oz. can tomato paste
- 36 oz. water (use the tomato paste can)
- 28 oz. can tomato puree
- 1 tsp. salt
- 1 tsp. brown sugar (I use Sugar in the Raw)
- 1 tsp. dried basil
- 1/2 tsp. dried oregano
- 1/2 tsp. dried tarragon

Direction

- Sauté minced garlic in olive oil until slightly browned.
- Add tomato paste.
- Add water; I find it easiest to start with small amounts of water and stirring well until the tomato paste is thinned down some.
- Add remaining ingredients in the order listed and mix well.
- Bring sauce mixture to a boil, then lower the heat and simmer *uncovered* for 90 minutes, stirring every 30 minutes. The sauce WILL spatter as it simmers; I use a screen designed to keep frying foods from spattering to reduce this. Do NOT use a pot lid; the sauce needs to cook down in quantity.
- This recipe makes a lot of sauce; it can be divided and frozen for later use.

9. Basic Tomato Sauce Recipe

Serving: 6 | Prep: | Cook: 90mins |Ready in:

Ingredients

- 1/4 cup extra-virgin olive oil
- 1 finely chopped small onion
- 2 minced garlic cloves
- 1 finely chopped stalk of celery
- 1 finely chopped carrot
- 3/4 teaspoon salt
- 1/4 teaspoon freshly ground black pepper
- 2 28-oz cans crushed tomatoes with juice
- 2 dried bay leaves

Direction

- Heat oil over medium high heat.
- Add onion and garlic and sauté until soft and translucent, about 5 to 10 minutes.
- Add celery, carrots and season with salt and pepper.
- Sauté until all the vegetables are soft, about 5 to 10 minutes.
- Add tomatoes and bay leaves and simmer uncovered on very low heat for 1 to 1-1/2 hours or until thick.
- Remove bay leaves and adjust the seasoning.
- Process until smooth, half of the tomato sauce in a food processor. Continue with remaining tomato sauce.
- Use the sauce as needed.
- Note: If not using all the sauce, allow it to cool completely and pour into freezer plastic bags. This will freeze up to 6 months.

10. Basil Tomato Sauce Recipe

Serving: 8 | Prep: | Cook: 16mins |Ready in:

Ingredients

- 1 tablespoon olive oil
- 1 large onion, chopped

- 2 cloves garlic, minced
- 28 ounces roma tomatoes, undrained
- 1/2 teaspoon sugar (optional)
- 1/4 teaspoon salt
- 1/2 teaspoon crushed red pepper (optional)
- 3 tablespoons fresh basil, julienned

Direction

- Sauté onion in olive oil until tender.
- Add minced garlic.
- Sauté 30 seconds more.
- Add tomatoes, sugar (if desired), red pepper and salt.
- Bring to a boil over medium heat.
- Reduce heat.
- Simmer, uncovered, for 10 to 15 minutes OR until desired consistency.
- Stir in basil.
- Cook 1 minute more.
- Makes three cups.

11. Buttery Alfredo Sauce

Serving: 6 | Prep: | Cook: 3hours | Ready in:

Ingredients

- 1 cup unsalted butter
- 1 ½ tablespoons minced garlic
- 1 tablespoon all-purpose flour
- 4 cups heavy cream
- ¼ cup whole milk
- 8 ounces freshly shredded Parmesan cheese
- 2 ounces shredded fontina cheese
- ½ teaspoon salt
- 1 teaspoon ground black pepper

Direction

- Melt the butter in a large pot over medium heat. Stir in the garlic and flour, and cook and stir until the garlic is fragrant but not browned, about 1 minute. Whisk in heavy cream and milk, whisking constantly until the

mixture is hot and slightly thickened, about 10 minutes. Gradually stir in the Parmesan cheese and fontina cheese. Season with salt and black pepper. Continue to simmer until the cheese has melted and the sauce is thickened, stirring often, 20 to 30 more minutes.
- Nutrition Facts
- Per Serving:
- 770.6 calories; protein 15.7g 31% DV; carbohydrates 6.2g 2% DV; fat 77.3g 119% DV; cholesterol 253.5mg 85% DV; sodium 735.5mg 29% DV.

12. Chicken And Pesto Pasta Recipe

Serving: 45 | Prep: | Cook: 30mins | Ready in:

Ingredients

- 3 chicken breast fillets
- lemon-pepper seasoning
- parsley flakes or fresh parsley
- freshly ground black pepper
- salt
- 4 Tbsp. extra virgin olive oil + 1/4 cup lemon juice
- 1 lbs. fusilli pasta (I recommend Ronzoni Smart pasta)
- 1 Jar Pre-made Pesto--I like Classico--(or, see below)
- 2-3 cloves garlic, crushed
- handful fresh basil
- 2-3 cups olive oil

Direction

- Chop chicken breasts into 1" cubes
- Season liberally with lemon-pepper, parsley, salt and pepper on both sides
- Set 1 large pot of salted water to boil, then cook pasta about 8 min.
- Combine olive oil & lemon juice thoroughly, then coat bottom of a large skillet and heat on medium high until oil begins to bubble

- Pan fry chicken in hot oil about 5 minutes each side (I pulled a piece off and cut in half to check for pink before finishing)
- Once pasta is ready, drain and pour into large bowl.
- If making pesto from scratch, add basil, garlic, and olive oil to food processor and pulse until smooth. Add pesto to hot pasta and toss to coat
- Add chicken to pasta, toss lightly, and serve

13. Chicken Chorizo Pasta With A Creamy Sauce Recipe

Serving: 6 | Prep: | Cook: 20mins | Ready in:

Ingredients

- 2 single chicken breast
- 3x chorizo sausage – sliced
- 400g penne pasta
- 50g butter
- 150g parmesan cheese – grated
- 50g extra parmesan cheese – grated
- 150ml milk
- 150ml Cream
- 3x tomatoes – deseeded & diced
- baby spinach
- salt & pepper
- parsley - chopped

Direction

- Char grill chicken & sausages. (Slice chicken before serving)
- Cook pasta as packet directions
- Place butter, milk & cream in a pan over low heat until butter is melted & well combined, remove from heat add parmesan cheese, salt & pepper stir until blended & smooth.
- Drain pasta, toss with baby spinach leaves & chorizo sausage mix through creamy sauce.
- Add tomato, Plate up pasta, top with sliced chicken, sprinkle with extra parmesan & parsley.

14. Chicken Fillets In Tomato Amp Wine Sauce Recipe

Serving: 4 | Prep: | Cook: 30mins | Ready in:

Ingredients

- 1 lb chicken breast fillets, cut in 8 pieces
- 1/2 tsp. coarse ground pepper
- 1/2 tsp. salt
- 1 (16 oz) can whole tomatoes, quartered with liquid
- 2 purple onions, sliced
- 2 garlic cloves
- 1 tsp basil
- 1/2 c. white wine
- Cooked fettucini

Direction

- Heat pan with butter to medium high. Brown chicken about 2 min each. Remove chicken, sprinkle with salt and pepper. Pour tomato liquid in fry pan with onion, garlic and basil. Bring to boil, reduce heat, cover and simmer 5 min until onion is tender. Add tomatoes, wine and chicken. Cover and simmer 15 min. Remove cover and cook on medium 5 minutes. Serve over fettuccini.

15. Chicken Fillets In Tomato And Wine Sauce Recipe

Serving: 4 | Prep: | Cook: 30mins | Ready in:

Ingredients

- 1 lb. chicken breast fillets, cut in 8 pieces
- 1/2 tsp. coarse ground pepper
- 1/2 tsp. salt

- 1 (16 oz) can whole tomatoes, quartered with liquid
- 2 purple onions,sliced
- 2 garlic gloves
- 1 tsp basil
- 1/2 c white wine
- Cooked Fettucini

Direction

- Heat pan with butter to medium high. Brown chicken about 2 min each. Remove chicken, sprinkle with salt and pepper. Pour tomato liquid in fry pan with onion, garlic and basil. Bring to boil, reduce heat, cover and simmer 5 min until onion is tender. Add tomatoes, wine and chicken. Cover and simmer 15 min. Remove cover and cook on medium 5 minutes. Serve over fettuccini.

16. Chicken Pasta With Blush Sauce Recipe

Serving: 62 | Prep: | Cook: 10mins | Ready in:

Ingredients

- Cooked chicken breast (grill or bake chicken even go one step further and marrinate it in Italian dressing)
- 1/2 lb asparagus
- 1/2 sweet onion
- lil or lot of crushed garlic
- mushroom pieces
- sun dried tomatoes
- 1 jar of marrinarra sauce
- 1 jar of alfedo sauce
- a garganchuan heaping spoon of pesto-basil
- 1 lb of pasta penne or bowtie!
- grated parmasean cheese

Direction

- Cook your pasta and set to the side

- Heat up and stir your 3 sauces together and set aside
- Chop the asparagus about 1/2 inch (you know bite size pieces)
- Dice your onion
- Have your shrooms ready and garlic and sun dried tomatoes (this is optional) be creative
- Any who sauté these in a pan with some Olive oil
- Do the onions and asparagus first since those take longer to sauté (common sense right) then the garlic and shrooms! Be creative add sum fresh cracked pepper and salt or oregano to the veggies
- Next throw in the chicken diced or sliced whatever floats your boat! Now for the sauce and cooked pasta~ mix that in! Learn how to sauté with the flip of the wrist! Don't use a spoon! You look really cool doing it and will impress your friends! Kind of like entertainment! Awe shucks sing some opera too!
- Add sum grated cheese at the last step so it melts just a bit!
- You can add more too after you serve! Kraft has a disposable parmesan cheese grater for like 5 bucks! And don't critique me on my spelling I am too full to do spell check, I just cooked and ate this dish!

17. Chicken Pesto Tortellini Recipe

Serving: 6 | Prep: | Cook: 20mins | Ready in:

Ingredients

- 1 lb. boneless, skinless chicken breast, cut into bite-size peices
- 1/2 lb. mushrooms, sliced thin
- 1/2 lb. smoked or pre-cooked ham, cubed (this is a great way to use up leftover holiday ham)
- 1 family size package totrellini
- 1 small tub pest sauce from the deli section, or about 1 1/2 C. if you make your own

- 1/2 C. frozen peas

Direction

- Bring enough water to a boil to cook the tortellini, and cook per directions.
- Heat a large skillet over medium-high heat. Drizzle in some olive oil and brown chicken.
- Once chicken is mostly browned, add mushrooms and ham and cook until the mushrooms begin to soften.
- Add frozen peas to the pan and cook over medium heat until soft.
- When tortellini is done, drain and add to the large skillet with the chicken mixture.
- Remove pan from heat and add pesto. Stir to combine.

18. Cilantro Pesto Recipe

Serving: 4 | Prep: | Cook: | Ready in:

Ingredients

- 2 cups, packed, of cilantro, large stems removed
- 1/2 cup blanched almonds (or walnuts or pecans)
- 1/4 cup chopped red onion
- 1/2 teaspoon chopped and seeded serrano chile
- 1/2 teaspoon salt
- 1/4 cup olive oil

Direction

- In a food processor, pulse the cilantro, almonds, onion, chili, and salt until well blended. With the food processor running, slowly add the olive oil in a steady stream.
- Add more oil as needed for your use.
- Makes about 1 cup

19. Coconut Pesto Recipe

Serving: 4 | Prep: | Cook: | Ready in:

Ingredients

- cilantro coconut pesto
- 1 cup fresh organic cilantro leaves- packed well into measuring cup
- 1 large clove garlic
- 6 tablespoons melted virgin coconut oil (or 3 coconut oil and 3 olive oil)
- 2 tablespoons fresh lemon juice
- 1 cup raw almonds or walnuts (or other nut of your choice- organic if possible)
- salt & pepper, optional

Direction

- Place cilantro and garlic in food processor and process until well chopped.
- Add coconut oil and process a few seconds until mixture is well blended and fairly smooth.
- Add nuts and lemon juice and process until fairly smooth and well blended.
- Also, if it is too thick for your liking - add small amounts of water until you are happy with it.
- I do not add salt- it does not need it- but you may add salt and pepper to taste if you wish.
- You may double this recipe and divide into two containers - it freezes well and is handy to have to flavor almost anything.

20. Curried Tomato And Spinach Sauce On Pasta Recipe

Serving: 1 | Prep: | Cook: 10mins | Ready in:

Ingredients

- 5 oz [wt] (1/2 of a 14.5 fl. oz can) diced tomatoes
- 1/4 cup water

- 1/2 tsp dried basil
- 1/2 tsp garam masala
- 1/2 tsp curry powder
- pinch cayenne pepper
- pinch cinnamon
- 2 cloves garlic, minced
- 3 oz (about 3 cups) baby spinach
- 3/4 cup fat free plain yogurt (I use Source)
- 1 cup cooked rice fettuccine

Direction

- In a medium saucepan combine tomatoes, water, basil, garam masala, curry powder, cayenne pepper, cinnamon and garlic. Bring to a brisk simmer and cook 5 minutes, stirring occasionally.
- Stir in spinach, cover the pot and simmer 4 minutes.
- Remove from heat, adjust seasoning to taste.
- Stir in yogurt and fettuccine, tossing well.
- Serve immediately.

21. Dried Tomato Pesto Recipe

Serving: 6 | Prep: | Cook: 10mins | Ready in:

Ingredients

- 1/2 cup dried tomatoes
- 1 2/3 cups broth (whatever your preference)
- 1/2 cup tightly packed sweet basil
- 1-2 cloves garlic
- 1/4 cup freshly grated Parmesan
- 1 tablespoon walnuts, toasted
- 2-3 teaspoons olive oil
- 1/4 teaspoon pepper
- 1/4 teaspoon salt

Direction

- Combine tomatoes and broth, bring to a boil.
- Remove from heat, cover, and let stand until softened (10-20 minutes.)

- Remove tomatoes, place in a food processor. Retain broth.
- Add remaining ingredients plus a few tablespoons of broth to processor.
- Process until smooth, stopping to scrap sides and add broth as necessary.
- Process until desired consistency.
- Refrigerate for 3 days or freeze for up to 3 months.
- Serve with bowties or other pasta with larger surfaces.
- Makes about 1 1/2 cups.

22. Drunken Veggie Pasta Sauce Recipe

Serving: 8 | Prep: | Cook: 45mins | Ready in:

Ingredients

- 5 garlic cloves - finely chopped
- 1 cup red wine (be generous!)
- 2 cups shredded zucchini (about 1 whole, peeled zucchini)
- 1 medium onion - chopped
- Two 14.5-oz cans of stewed tomatoes - Italian style
- Two 14.5-oz cans of tomato sauce - Italian style
- 7-oz. can tomato paste
- 1 Tbl. kosher salt
- 1/2 Tbl. black pepper
- 1/2 tsp. crushed red pepper
- 1 Tbl. sugar
- 6 oz fresh spinach
- 1 medium green pepper - chopped

Direction

- Pour about 1/2 cup of the red wine in a large, deep sauté pan.
- Add the garlic and sauté for 5 minutes over medium to med-high heat.
- Add the onion and zucchini. Pour in the rest of the wine. Stir well and cook for about another 5-7 minutes, stirring often.

- Add the next 6 ingredients (through sugar) and stir well. Lower the heat (to medium) to maintain a simmer for about 10-15 minutes, stirring occasionally. (As the sauce cooks, you may want to cut some of the larger chunks of the stewed tomatoes as they become tenderer.)
- Stir in the spinach and green pepper and continue to simmer for about 15-20 minutes, stirring occasionally.

23. EASY GREEK PASTA SAUCE Recipe

Serving: 4 | Prep: | Cook: 20mins | Ready in:

Ingredients

- 1 1/2 LBS CHOPMEAT
- 1 DICED MEDIUM onion
- 3 cloves GARLIC- MINCED
- 1/2 TEASPOON cinnamon
- 2 JARS (YOUR CHOICE)PREMADE pasta sauce
- 1 LB pasta OF CHOICE
- PARMASAN cheese(OPTIONAL)

Direction

- PLACE WATER IN POT FOR PASTA. BEGIN THE HEATING PROCESS!
- BROWN YOUR CHOPMEAT, ONION, AND GARLIC IN A LARGE FRYING PAN ONCE THE MEAT IS BROWN, DRAIN. ADD THE CINNAMON AND 2 JARS OF SAUCE AND SIMMER FOR ABOUT 10 MINUTES MORE
- ADD YOUR SALT AND PASTA TO THE BOILING POT OF WATER. COOK 12 MINUTES AND DRAIN.
- SERVE SAUCE OVER PASTA.TOP WITH CHEESE (OPTIONAL)
- SERVE WITH A NICE SALAD (GREEK?!) AND SOME NICE CRUSTY ITALIAN BREAD

24. Easy Marinara A Plenty Recipe

Serving: 8 | Prep: | Cook: 1hours | Ready in:

Ingredients

- 4T olive oil
- 1/2 medium onion, diced
- 1 bell pepper, diced
- 8oz fresh mushrooms, chopped
- 4 cloves garlic, minced
- 1 28oz can tomato puree(thicker than sauce)
- 1 28oz can crushed tomatoes
- total of about 1/4 cup chopped fresh Italian herbs OR can sub 2T dried
- kosher or sea salt and fresh ground black pepper
- 1t baking soda(optional) OR
- 1T sugar(optional)
- 5-6 links specialty, fully or partially cooked sausage, sliced(Italian, Sundried Tomato, Spinach/Asiago, etc)(Optional)

Direction

- Sauté onion, bell pepper, mushrooms and garlic in olive oil over medium heat until onion is tender, about 10 minutes.
- In large soup pan, or 2-3 quart slow cooker, combine remaining ingredients then add the onion/garlic mixture. Simmer over medium/low heat, OR set slow cooker to high and cook 45 min-1 hour, stirring occasionally.
- Serve over favorite cooked pasta.
- **the sugar or baking soda can be used, if desired, to help balance the acidity of the sauce. I, personally, don't use sugar.

25. Easy Spaghetti Meat Sauce Recipe

Serving: 6 | Prep: | Cook: 45mins | Ready in:

Ingredients

- 1 and 1/2 lbs of ground beef
- 2 cans of tomato paste
- 2 cans of tomato sauce
- 2 tsp each of the following:
- oregano
- garlic salt
- italian seasoning
- marjoram
- onion powder
- basil
- rosemary
- to taste:
- red pepper flakes
- 1/3 cup of sugar
- (Being a poor college kid I know that sometimes that it may be hard to get all those spices in one place. The three important ones are the garlic salt italian seasoning and the sugar. If you missing the rest, just add more Itallian seasoning!)

Direction

- Open your cans of sauces and dump them in your crock pot. Then take a whisk, (or a fork whichever is handy) and mix in thoroughly the tomato paste Throw in your spices and give it a quick mix. Now with salt and pepper brown your 1 and 1/2 lbs. of Ground Beef, when it's cooked thoroughly, drain any excess fat and throw it in the crock pot with a quick stir. I suggest you let it cook for at least 45 min but the longer it sits and stews, the better. Be sure to try it again the second day, it's even better!

26. Easy Spaghetti Sauce Recipe

Serving: 8 | Prep: | Cook: 45mins | Ready in:

Ingredients

- 1 lb ground beef
- 4 cloves garlic, finely chopped
- 1 onion, peeled and diced

- 2 cups of button mushrooms, finely chopped
- 2 tbsp tomato paste
- 1/2 tsp dried chili flakes (optional)
- 1 bay leaf
- 1/4 cup red wine (optional)
- 1/2 cup water
- 1 can of crushed tomatoes (I use one that is flavored with roasted garlic)
- 1/2 tsp each of dried thyme, oregano, basil
- 1/2 cup fresh flat leaf parsley, chopped
- 1/2 cup parmesan cheese, finely grated
- Drizzle of olive oil when serving

Direction

- In a Dutch oven, break up beef with a whisk (this is an easier way to break down meat versus using a wooden spoon).
- Let cook for 5-7 minutes. Drain fat off.
- Add garlic and onion. Sweat for a couple of minutes.
- Add mushrooms and season with salt and pepper. Sweat for about 6-8 minutes.
- Add herbs and tomato paste and wine. Cook for a couple of minutes.
- Add crushed tomatoes and water. (This is when I also added in the sundried tomatoes in my variation)
- Simmer on low heat for about 25 minutes. Add cheese.
- Remove bay leaf and serve over cooked pasta. Dust with more cheese, hit with a fine drizzle of olive oil and some more chopped fresh parsley for garnish.

27. Easy Spinach And Cheese Pasta Sauce Recipe

Serving: 6 | Prep: | Cook: 10mins | Ready in:

Ingredients

- 16 oz. penne, Rotini, or other short pasta
- 8 oz. cream cheese
- 3 oz. goat cheese

- 4 cloves of garlic
- 2-3 Handfuls of fresh spinach leafs
- thyme
- parmesan cheese
- salt
- pepper
- extra virgin olive oil

Direction

- Start your pasta water boiling.
- While waiting for the pasta water to boil, get your food processor.
- Add the Cream Cheese, Goat Cheese, Garlic and Spinach to the food processor and combine it. (Drizzle the Olive Oil in as needed to achieve your desired consistency. It is a matter of personal taste.)
- If you are using dried Thyme, add the Thyme to the food processor mixture.
- Salt and Pepper to taste.
- Once pasta is cooked, drain and DO NOT RINSE. Rinsing the pasta will remove the starch from its surface and will not allow the sauce to stick as well.
- Combine drained pasta with sauce in a bowl and serve. I find that about 1/2 to 3/4 cup of the sauce mixture is sufficient for a 16 oz. package of Pasta. Do not commit the mistake us Americans so often make by over-saucing your pasta.
- You can top it off with grilled chicken and Parmesan if you so desire.

28. Easy Pasta Sauce Recipe

Serving: 6 | Prep: | Cook: 60mins | Ready in:

Ingredients

- *For basic sauce
- About 10 ripe tomatoes
- clove or two of garlic
- Pinch of salt
- Pinch of pepper

- basil
- oregano
- olive oil
- vinegar
- *Other possible ingredients
- Coco-Chile spice blend
- onions
- spinach

Direction

- Wash the tomatoes and pull off the stems. In a large pot pour a generous amount of olive oil into the pan. Cut tomatoes in half and put them into the pot. Turn on the burner to very low and cover pot. As the tomatoes start to cook, dice at least one full garlic clove and put into the pot along with salt and pepper.
- As the tomatoes cook, occasionally smash them with a potato smasher or any utensil. You will do this many times until it gets smooth. After about 25 minutes of cooking add a generous amount of basil and about half that amount of oregano. Put in a few splashes of vinegar. I will also sometimes add Chili spice, onions, mushrooms, cherry tomatoes and/or spinach.
- When you smashed a few times it will get watery. Continue smashing and cooking it at very low until it becomes your desired thickness.

29. Eggplant And Olive Pasta Sauce Recipe

Serving: 3 | Prep: | Cook: 20mins | Ready in:

Ingredients

- 6 Tbl extra virgin olive oil
- 1 small eggplant (about 1 lb) trimmed, peeled, and cut into 1/2 inch cubes
- 1 small (6 oz) can tomato paste
- 1/4 cup chopped green olives
- 1 Tbl capers, rinsed and drained

- 1 Tbl fresh basil, chopped
- 1 Tbl fresh parsley, chopped
- 2 tsp red wine vinegar
- 1/2 tsp salt
- black pepper to taste
- pinch of sugar

Direction

- Heat 4 tbsp. olive oil in large skillet over medium high heat, add eggplant. Sauté, stirring constantly, until eggplant is tender and browned, about 10 minutes. Drain on paper towels.
- Add remaining 2 tbsp. oil to skillet. Stir in eggplant, tomato paste, olives, capers, basil, parsley, vinegar, salt, pepper, and sugar. Cover and simmer 5 minutes. Toss hot pasta with sauce and serve immediately.

30. Elaines Spaghetti Sauce Recipe

Serving: 12 | Prep: | Cook: 120mins | Ready in:

Ingredients

- 1 can unsalted tomato paste
- ½ each of green, orange, red, yellow sweet pepper, finely chopped
- 1 large can diced tomatoes, or 6 large, fresh, diced
- ½ lb. lean ground beef
- ½ lb lean ground pork
- ½ lb lean ground turkey
- 6 – 8 shallots, finely chopped
- 2 whole bay leaves
- 2 cloves garlic, minced
- approx 3 tbsp soya sauce
- approx 1 – ½ cups dry red wine
- approx 3 large stalks celery, finely chopped
- approx 3 medium carrots, finely chopped
- 3 garlic cloves, finely chopped
- salt & pepper to taste
- oregano & basil, a good pinch of each

Direction

- In a large saucepan, combine the meats. Add about 2 tbsp. extra virgin olive oil.
- Add the shallots. Lightly brown the mixture, cooking until the shallots are nicely caramelized.
- Transfer to large pot, and add:
- Diced peppers
- Diced tomatoes
- Soya sauce
- Red wine
- Celery and carrots
- Garlic
- Bay leaves
- Oregano and basil, salt & pepper
- Cook on medium heat, stirring frequently.
- Reduce heat to simmer, and reduce the sauce to thicken.
- Remove bay leaves.
- Serve over spaghetti, topped with grated Parmesan, or cheese of your choice, garnished with fresh parsley leaf.
- Garlic bread goes really well with this dish, as does a fresh, tossed salad.

31. Faith Fairchilds Pesto Recipe

Serving: 4 | Prep: | Cook: | Ready in:

Ingredients

- fresh basil leaves
- garlic cloves
- olive oil
- salt
- pepper
- OPTIONAL:
- pine nuts
- parmesan cheese, grated.

Direction

- Tear the basil into small pieces.
- Chop several cloves of garlic into small pieces.

- Place all the ingredients in a blender and puree until mostly smooth.
- May be frozen.
- There are regular and special versions of prepared pesto sauce that can be found in specialty markets.

32. Fast And Easy Pasta With Tomato Shrimp Sauce Recipe

Serving: 6 | Prep: | Cook: 25mins | Ready in:

Ingredients

- 1 28-ounce can tomatoes
- 1 medium onion, chopped
- 1/2 teaspoon coarsely ground chili
- 2 teaspoons fresh basil, chopped
- 3 tablespoons fresh parsley, chopped
- 2 tablespoons olive oil
- 2 cloves garlic, minced
- 1 pound linguine pasta
- 1/2 pound shrimp, peeled and deveined
- grated romano cheese to taste

Direction

- Purée tomatoes in food processor and place in a saucepan. Add onion, chili, basil, parsley, olive oil and garlic. Simmer on low for 20 minutes. Add shrimp and simmer until pink, approximately 3 minutes. Cook and drain pasta. Serve shrimp sauce over pasta. Sprinkle with Romano cheese.

33. Fettuccine Pesto Recipe

Serving: 6 | Prep: | Cook: 5mins | Ready in:

Ingredients

- 1 cup fresh basil leaves
- 3/4 cup olive oil

- 1/4 cup grated parmesan cheese
- 1 tsp minced garlic
- 1 tbls. pine nuts
- 1/2 tsp salt
- 1/4 tsp. ground pepper
- 12 oz. fettuccine

Direction

- Add 1st 7 ingredients to a blender or processor and process until smooth.
- Cook fettuccine in 6-8 qts. boiling water until al dente. About 5 minutes
- Drain pasta, reserving 2 tbsp. of its water
- Add water to pesto and blend
- Toss hot fettuccine with pesto.

34. Fettuccine With Cilantro Pesto Sauce Recipe

Serving: 6 | Prep: | Cook: 20mins | Ready in:

Ingredients

- 1 pound fettuccine
- 16 ounces black beans rinsed
- 11 ounce can Mexican style corn drained
- Pesto:
- 2 cups fresh cilantro
- 2 cups fresh parsley
- 4 ounces green chilies drained
- 1/3 cup unsalted roasted peanuts
- 1/4 cup fresh lime juice
- 2 tablespoons olive oil
- 1 tablespoon bottled chopped garlic in oil
- 1/2 teaspoon ground cumin
- 1/2 teaspoon salt

Direction

- Cook pasta according to directions.
- Puree pesto ingredients in food processor until smooth.
- With processor running gradually add 1/3 cup pasta cooking water.

- Drain pasta then return to pot and add pesto, black beans and corn.
- Toss to mix and heat through.

35. Five Minute Tomato Sauce Recipe

Serving: 4 | Prep: | Cook: 4mins | Ready in:

Ingredients

- 1/4 cup extra virgin olive oil
- 1 1/2 tsp crushed red pepper flakes
- 1/2 tsp fine grain sea salt
- 3 medium cloves of garlic, finely chopped
- 1 28-oz can crushed red tomatoes (plain)
- zest of one lemon

Direction

- Combine the olive oil, red pepper flakes, sea salt, and garlic in a cold saucepan.
- Stir while you heat the saucepan over medium-high heat, sauté just 45 seconds or so until everything is fragrant - you don't want the garlic to brown.
- Stir in the tomatoes and heat to a gentle simmer, this takes just a couple minutes.
- Remove from heat and carefully take a taste (you don't want to burn your tongue)...If the sauce needs more salt add it now.
- Stir in the lemon zest reserving a bit to sprinkle on top of your pasta.
- Makes about a quart of tomato sauce.

36. Fresh Tomato Sauce With Ricotta Recipe

Serving: 2 | Prep: | Cook: 15mins | Ready in:

Ingredients

- 2 Tbl extra virgin olive oil
- 1 garlic clove, crushed
- 1 and 1/2 cups chopped fresh ripe tomatoes (about 1 lb)
- 2 Tbl chopped fresh basil
- 1 Tbl chopped fresh parsley
- 1/4 tsp dried oregano
- 1/8 tsp dried thyme
- 1 cup ricotta cheese
- salt and pepper to taste
- freshly grated parmesan cheese

Direction

- Heat oil in medium skillet over low heat, stir in garlic, sauté 1 minute. Add tomatoes. Simmer, uncovered, until mixture boils and begins to thicken, about 10 minutes. Add basil, parsley, oregano, and thyme; whisk in Ricotta cheese until blended well. Heat, stirring, about 1 minute. Add salt and pepper to taste. Toss with hot pasta, serve with Parmesan cheese.

37. Garden Of Eden Pasta Sauce Recipe

Serving: 4 | Prep: | Cook: 15mins | Ready in:

Ingredients

- 2 Large tomatoes, cored and chopped
- 1 yellow or orange bell pepper, seeded and chopped
- 1 medium cucumber, peeled, seeded, and chopped
- 8 ounces fresh mozzarella cheese, cut into 1/2-inch chunks
- 2 scallions, sliced thin
- 1/2 c. chopped fresh basil
- 1 t. salt
- 1/2 c. extra-virgin olive oil
- 2 T. red wine vinegar
- 1 garlic clove, minced
- 1/2 t. ground cumin
- 1/2 t. dried oregano

Direction

- Combine tomatoes, bell pepper, cucumber, cheese, scallions, basil, and salt in large bowl. Whisk oil, vinegar, garlic, cumin, and oregano in small bowl. Pour oil mixture over tomato mixture and toss to coat. Cover and let stand at room temperature 1 hour.
- Toss tomato mixture with cooked pasta and reserved pasta cooking water, if necessary. Serve.

38. Homemade Pasta Sauce

Serving: 6 | Prep: | Cook: | Ready in:

Ingredients

- 1 medium onion, chopped
- 10 fresh baby carrots, diced
- 1 tablespoon olive oil
- 3 garlic cloves, minced
- 2 cans (14-1/2 ounces each) diced tomatoes, undrained
- 1 can (14-1/2 ounces) chicken broth
- 1 can (6 ounces) tomato paste
- 1 teaspoon dried oregano
- 1 teaspoon dried basil
- 1/2 teaspoon salt
- Hot cooked pasta

Direction

- In a large saucepan, heat oil over medium heat. Add onions, mushrooms, zucchini, and garlic. Cook and stir until tender, about 5 minutes.
- Add lentils and 3 cups water to vegetables. Bring to a rolling boil, stirring occasionally. Reduce heat to low, cover, and cook 45 to 60 minutes.
- Stir in tomato sauce, tomato paste, sugar, and 1/2 cup water. Bring to a boil. Reduce heat, cover, and simmer for 20 minutes. If necessary, add more water to keep the sauce from sticking. Be careful not to dilute; the sauce should be quite thick.
- Nutrition Facts
- Per Serving:
- 145 calories; protein 8.9g 18% DV; carbohydrates 25.5g 8% DV; fat 1.8g 3% DV; cholesterolmg; sodium 466.1mg 19% DV.

39. Homemade Tomato Sauce With Fettucine Noodles And Meatless Meat Recipe

Serving: 2 | Prep: | Cook: 15mins | Ready in:

Ingredients

- > Your favorite noodles (I used fettuccine.)
- > Petite diced tomatoes
- > garlic
- > oregano
- > basil
- > Morningstar Farms or Boca meatless meat crumbles
- > Reduced fat parmesan cheese

Direction

- Sautee tomatoes, garlic, oregano and basil in a pan.
- Prepare noodles to package instructions.
- Add "meat" to the sauce to heat.
- Sprinkle cheese on top (optional)
- Garnish with dried/fresh parsley or basil.

40. Hot Dog Spicy Meat Sauce Recipe

Serving: 10 | Prep: | Cook: 60mins | Ready in:

Ingredients

- 2 lbs ground beef

- 1 vidalia onion, diced fine
- 3 cloves garlic, chopped
- 2 chipotles (from can with adobo sauce)
- 1 tbsp worcester sauce
- 3 tbsp cider vinegar
- 2 28oz cans crushed tomatos
- 1 tbsp cumin
- 1 tbsp mustard powder
- 1 tbsp chili powder
- 1 tbsp cayenne pepper
- 2 tbsp adobo sauce (from above can)

Direction

- Sauté ground beef and onion over medium high heat in a large heavy bottomed pot
- Once meat loses pink, add garlic and chipotles
- Add rest of ingredients, bring just to a boil then reduce heat to a simmer
- Simmer, uncovered, for about an hour, stirring occasionally. Sauce should thicken slightly
- Serve over whatever's around... especially hot dogs on toasted buns

41. Italian Pasta Sauce Super Easy Super Tasty Recipe

Serving: 8 | Prep: | Cook: 240mins | Ready in:

Ingredients

- 2 lb. hot italian sausage (substitute for sweet if you don't like spicy)
- 1 large onion (diced)
- 2 garlic cloves (minced)
- 2 packages mushrooms (diced)
- 2 teaspoons dried oregano
- 2 teaspoons dried thyme
- 1 large (32oz.) can of tomatoes (crushed, whole, diced - either one would work)
- 1 cup fresh basil OR 1 tablespoon of dryed basil
- 1 cup Italian parsley

Direction

- In a big pan sauté an onion, garlic and smashed hot Italian sausage (taken out of their casings) until cooked.
- Add mushrooms, oregano and thyme and cook for another 5 minutes.
- Meanwhile put half of the tomatoes from the can in a blender and blend for just a few seconds.
- Add it to the pan. Do the same with the rest of the tomatoes.
- Add fresh herbs.
- Bring to a boil and reduce the heat to simmer.
- Let it simmer for 4 hours, stirring occasionally.
- Mix it with noodles or penne, sprinkle with parmesan cheese and enjoy! And don't forget that tomatoes are packed with vitamin C and will help you prevent heart disease and avoid prostate cancer for your hunny!

42. Italian Spaghetti Sauce Recipe

Serving: 810 | Prep: | Cook: 240mins | Ready in:

Ingredients

- 2 1/2 lb. Hot or sweet Italian sausage
- 3 cloves garlic
- 1 medium onion - chopped
- salt and pepper to taste
- oregano - 1 tbls.
- 4 or 5 20 oz. cans tomato puree
- 1 tbls. sugar

Direction

- IN A LARGE DEEP SAUCEPAN
- Sauté' sausage and onion until sausage is browned and onion is opaque. Turn off heat.
- Add tomato puree with sausage and onion. Season with salt and pepper and oregano
- Add sugar and stir
- Cook on low flame for 4 to 4 1/2 hours. Stir at different intervals.

43. Lentils And Rice With Tangy Tomato Sauce Recipe

Serving: 8 | Prep: | Cook: 60mins |Ready in:

Ingredients

- 2 cups uncooked brown rice
- 1 pound lentils
- 2 tablespoons vegetable oil divided
- 1 tablespoon crushed garlic
- 32 ounces canned tomato sauce
- 1/2 cup water
- 1/4 cup white vinegar
- 1 teaspoon salt
- 1 medium white onion

Direction

- Cook rice according to directions then rinse lentils and put in pot covering with water.
- Bring to a boil and simmer on low 45 minutes.
- To make sauce sauté garlic in 1 tablespoon oil until golden then add tomato sauce.
- Simmer 15 minutes then add water and vinegar and bring to a boil.
- Remove from heat immediately and add salt.
- Finally slice onion in thin small pieces and sauté in remaining oil until brown and crispy.
- Arrange a layer of lentils on the bottom of a serving dish then follow with a layer of rice.
- Continue layering until all rice and lentils are used.
- Sprinkle onions and sauce on top before serving.

44. Light Pesto And Angel Hair Recipe

Serving: 4 | Prep: | Cook: 10mins |Ready in:

Ingredients

- Ingredients:
- ½ pkg (12oz) angel hair pasta
- ½ cup fresh basil leaves, rinsed and drained
- ½ cup water
- 1/3 cup nonfat grated parmesan cheese
- 3 Tbs. pine nuts
- 1 Tbs. chicken-flavor Bouillon Granules
- 1tsp. Minced garlic

Direction

- 1) Boil Angel Hair pasta as directed on the package.
- 2) Combine in a blender or food processor fresh basil leaves, water non-fat grated Parmesan cheese, pine nuts, chicken bouillon granules and minced garlic. Process until basil is finely chopped.
- 3) Place the angel hair pasta in a medium bowl, toss the processed mixture with the pasta.
- 4) Use Grated Parmesan to garnish. Serve.

45. Linguini With Vodka And Rosy Tomato Sauce Recipe

Serving: 4 | Prep: | Cook: 20mins |Ready in:

Ingredients

- 2 tablespoons olive oil
- 3 tablespoons butter
- 1 small white onion chopped
- 1 clove garlic minced
- 28 ounce can chunky tomato sauce
- 1 tablespoon fresh basil minced
- 1/8 teaspoon dried pepper flakes
- 1/2 cup vodka
- 1/2 cup heavy cream
- 3 tablespoons parmigiano reggiano grated
- 12 ounce linguini
- 1 teaspoon freshly ground black pepper
- Chopped cilantro

Direction

- Combine oil and butter in a medium skillet and sauté the onion for about 5 minutes.
- And garlic and sauté for one additional minute.
- Add all other ingredients except cream and pasta.
- After simmering for about 15 minutes add cream and reduce heat to keep it hot but not boiling.
- Cook pasta according to package directions and drain well.
- Spread a layer of sauce on a heated serving platter then pile on the pasta and top with the remaining sauce and garnish with chopped cilantro.

46. Lisas Spaghetti Sauce Italian Gravy Recipe

Serving: 30 | Prep: | Cook: 270mins | Ready in:

Ingredients

- 3 - 28 oz cans Tuttoroso tomato puree
- 2 - 18 oz cans Hunt's tomato paste
- 1 pkg country style spare ribs or sweet or hot sausage
- 3-4 lg. onions, sliced thin then cut in half
- 1-2 T. fresh minced garlic (I use quite a bit cause I love garlic)
- 4 bay leaves
- 1/4 - 1/2 cup basil (to your taste)
- 3/4 cup sugar
- 1/4 cup salt (its a BIG pot)
- fresh ground pepper to taste
- 3/4 cup grated romano cheese
- 1 1/2 cans water, use the puree can
- olive oil to cover bottom of pot

Direction

- In 16 qt. pot, brown meat, onions and garlic in olive oil.
- Remove meat to bowl.

- Add puree, paste and water. Whisk until smooth.
- Add all seasonings and cheese. Whisk again.
- Add meat back to pot. Bring to a low simmer.
- Simmer 4-5 hr. BUT I simmered mine for 2 hrs. on Sunday and it still came out great.
- Add more water as it cooks if you want a thinner sauce--(I like mine really thick-MIL likes hers thin)

47. Macs Easy Chilli Mushroom Pesto Pasta Recipe

Serving: 2 | Prep: | Cook: 10mins | Ready in:

Ingredients

- pasta (as much as you like)
- 2x tinned chopped tomatoes
- 1 green pepper
- 1 red chilli
- 6 mushrooms
- 1x garlic glove
- Handfull mangetout
- 2x teaspoon of red pesto
- salt'n'pepper
- Cooker (haha)

Direction

- Boil some water, put some salt in it, then pasta.
- Cut up veg, and crush garlic.
- Put the tinned tomatoes in a saucepan, mix the red pesto in, and put on low heat.
- Chuck the veg in and stir.
- When pasta cooked, drain and pour into the sauce. Mix the sauce in properly.
- Serve on a plate, and Eat!

48. Mommys Spaghetti Sauce Recipe

Serving: 8 | Prep: | Cook: 140mins | Ready in:

Ingredients

- 1 large onion -- diced
- 5 hot Italian sausages (I prefer hot Italian turkey sausage)
- olive oil
- 6 cloves pressed garlic
- 2 29oz. cans tomato sauce
- 2 29oz. cans tomato paste
- 2 tbsp oregano

Direction

- Fry diced onion in olive oil until partially soft.
- Remove sausage from casing and brown with onion.
- Add garlic and continue to fry until onion is cooked and sausage is browned
- Add tomato sauce, tomato paste, and oregano.
- Stir and simmer for 1-2 hours
- Taste test and adjust spices -- I never measure spices. I just add them as needed until it tastes right
- Serve with pasta
- This sauce is more flavorful the second day so make a day ahead if you like!

49. My Favorite Pesto With Lemon Zest Recipe

Serving: 6 | Prep: | Cook: | Ready in:

Ingredients

- 2 bucnches of fresh basil, about 3 - 3 1/2 cups leaves
- 2 medium cloves of garlic or 1 huge one
- 2 TBSP parsley
- 1/2 cup extra virgin olive oil
- 1/2 cup freshly grated parmesan cheese

- grated zest of 1 large lemon
- 1 TBSP pignoli nuts

Direction

- Put all of the ingredients in the work bowl of the food processor and blend until the desired consistency.

50. Nasturtium Pesto Recipe

Serving: 6 | Prep: | Cook: | Ready in:

Ingredients

- 4 C packed nasturtium leaves
- 3 – 5 cloves of garlic
- 1 ½ C extra virgin olive oil
- 2 drops Tabasco sauce
- 1 C walnuts

Direction

- Put all the ingredients into a food processor and blend until smooth.

51. Neapolitana Sauce And Pasta For Two Recipe

Serving: 2 | Prep: | Cook: 30mins | Ready in:

Ingredients

- 2 tbsp of good extra virgin olive oil
- 1 large onion, sliced and diced
- ½ tspn of freshly ground black pepper
- 3 cloves of garlic, pressed
- 6 whole anchovies
- 3 pieces of prosciutto, diced
- 6 medium sized roma tomatoes, diced
- 3 tbsp of concentrated tomato paste
- 200 grams (7 ounces) of spaghetti (per 2 persons)

Direction

- Put a large pot of water on the stove and turn heat up to high. Add a dash of salt and allow the water to boil.
- Put on a separate large saucepan (that will allow you to simmer and stir the end sauce without spillage) onto another part of the stove. Add oil, and onions and fry gently until they are translucent, add ground pepper and turn up heat for a minute or so.
- Add freshly pressed Garlic, Anchovies and Prosciutto. Turn down heat to medium and stir the pot for the next 3 – 5 minutes (this will break up the Anchovies leaving only the taste).
- Add diced Tomatoes, put on a firm fitting lid and allow the mixture to combine through gentle simmering for 5 minutes.
- Add concentrated Tomato paste.
- Into the other pot where you should now have the water boiling rapidly add 200 grams (7 ounces) of spaghetti and boil for about 9 or 10 minutes.
- When spaghetti is al dente turn heat off both pots and add spaghetti with tongs directly to the sauce.
- Stir and serve immediately with some good Italian bread (penne de casa is perfect).

52. Old Fashioned Spaghetti Sauce Recipe

Serving: 6 | Prep: | Cook: 480mins | Ready in:

Ingredients

- One pound spicy italian sausage
- One large white onion, chopped
- Five cloves garlic, chopped
- One large green bell pepper, chopped
- Two cups sliced crimini mushrooms
- One large can crushed tomatoes
- One large can tomato sauce
- One medium can tomato paste

- extra virgin olive oil
- red wine
- salt & pepper
- One tablespoon oregano
- Two large bay leaves
- spaghetti noodles
- Fresh parmesan or asiago cheese, grated

Direction

- Heat about two tablespoons of olive oil in a large, heavy skillet over medium-high heat. Remove sausage from casings and chop roughly. Brown in the olive oil. While sausage is cooking, sauté onion and garlic in three tablespoons olive oil in a large pot. When sausage is completely cooked, drain and add to onion and garlic. Add tomatoes, bell pepper, and mushrooms. Stir thoroughly and bring to a boil. Add red wine to desired consistency and taste. Add oregano and bay leaves, and salt and pepper to taste. Reduce heat, cover, and simmer all day, stirring occasionally. Remove bay leaves before serving. Serve over hot cooked spaghetti and top with cheese.
- Recipe is easy to double

53. One Pot Spaghetti With Meat Sauce Recipe

Serving: 4 | Prep: | Cook: 15mins | Ready in:

Ingredients

- 1 lb. ground turkey (or very lean ground beef)
- 2 cloves garlic, minced
- 2 c. water
- 1 28 - oz. jar/can spaghetti sauce
- 8 oz. uncooked spaghetti, broken into thirds

Direction

- Brown meat with garlic. Do not drain.

- Stir in water and spaghetti sauce. Bring to a boil.
- Stir in spaghetti.
- Boil 15 min., stirring occasionally.
- Variation: Cook 1 cup chopped green pepper and one chopped onion with garlic and ground turkey. May also add red pepper flakes.
- Ragu or Hunt's Traditional Spaghetti Sauce works well with this. Mushrooms would probably be a good addition.

54. Pamelas Semi Homemade Pasta Sauce Recipe

Serving: 6 | Prep: | Cook: 30mins | Ready in:

Ingredients

- EVOO
- 1/2 green bell pepper, chopped
- 1/2 red bell pepper, chopped
- 1/2 yellow onion, chopped
- handful fresh mushrooms, chopped (opt)
- 1 carrot chopped (opt)
- 1 celery stalk, chopped (opt)
- 3 cloves garlic, minced
- Dash of kosher salt and pepper
- tsp basil
- tsp parsley
- tsp oregano
- tsp thyme
- 1/2 cup red wine
- 1 jar pasta sauce (or your own simple tomato sauce)
- (ground meat is optional, sometimes I add it and sometimes I don't)

Direction

- In medium stockpot, sauté first 6 veggies in EVOO, until soft
- You can use any additional veggies you like...or have on hand

- Add garlic
- Add dash kosher salt and pepper
- Add herbs
- Sauté for 1 minute
- Turn up heat and add red wine
- Cook for 1 minute
- Add pasta sauce
- (I use Hunts original, because it is simple, tomato sauce, but you can use any jarred sauce, or make your own)
- *I usually let it simmer 2 hours over very low heat, but once the sauce is warmed through it is ready. It gets better the longer you let it simmer!
- **serve over pasta, or any Italian dish of your choice
- ***It's also wonderful to make with ground beef and Italian sausage mixed in, served over wheat pasta!
- As you can see it has many variations! Enjoy!

55. Pasta In A Smokey Bacon Tomato And Basil Sauce Recipe

Serving: 2 | Prep: | Cook: 20mins | Ready in:

Ingredients

- 6 rashers lean smokey bacon trimmed & cubed
- Tbsp olive oil
- 1 tin chopped tomatoes (400g)
- 3 cloves smoked garlic, crushed
- 1/2 onion, medium diced
- 4 button mushrooms, sliced
- Tsp hot chilli powder
- 1 chicken stock cube
- 2 Tsp tomato puree
- 2 Tsp caster sugar
- salt & pepper
- Handful fresh basil, chopped
- 150g Brown pasta
- For the garlic bread
- 1 ciabatta bread, halved
- 50g butter

- 4 cloves garlic
- tomato chutney
- 50g mature red cheddar grated

Direction

- (1) Boil pan of water for pasta.
- (2) Add olive oil in a medium sized pan then add bacon & onion cook for 5 mins.
- (3) Add chopped tomatoes, mushrooms & crushed garlic & bring to the boil.
- Add chicken stock cube, chilli powder, tomato puree, sugar & basil and leave to simmer for 15 mins.
- (4) Add salt & pepper to season.
- (5) Drain pasta & stir into sauce.
- (6) Serve in a bowl.
- Garlic Ciabatta with Tomato Chutney & Red Cheddar
- (1) Crush garlic & add to melted butter.
- (2) Brush garlic butter onto both sides of Ciabatta.
- (3) Spread tomato chutney onto garlic bread then top with grated cheese & put under grill until it is golden.

56. Pasta In Pesto Broth Recipe

Serving: 2 | Prep: | Cook: 10mins | Ready in:

Ingredients

- whole wheat pasta (I chose penne-orecchiette would be great- anything that will hold liquid...so it could also be small shells- but not spaghetti or anything long)
- pesto - I make my own
- frozen peas
- a block of parmigiano cheese

Direction

- Cook pasta in salted water on high heat according to package direction.

- Add some frozen peas to pasta about 1/2 way through cooking.
- Drain pasta/peas and reserve about 1-2 cups of the cooking liquid.
- Divide pasta and peas into 2 large bowls.
- Add a scoop of pesto and some cooking liquid and toss- pesto will combine with water to make a delicious broth.
- Using the big side of a box grater, shred some cheese on top and stir again to give the cheese a chance to melt slightly.
- Enjoy!

57. Pasta Pesto And Potatoes Recipe

Serving: 8 | Prep: | Cook: 20mins | Ready in:

Ingredients

- 3 medium red potatoes; unpeeled
- 8 ounces linguine
- 1 cup frozen green beans
- 3 tablespoons olive oil
- 1 cup pesto sauce
- 1/4 cup Parmesan cheese; grated
- salt and pepper; to taste

Direction

- Bring 4 quarts of water to boil in large pot.
- Add potatoes, cut into chunks, and cook over medium-high heat for about 5 minutes.
- Add frozen green beans, cook for 3 minutes.
- Add pasta, cook, uncovered, 8 to 10 minutes or until pasta is al dente and potatoes are done.
- Drain, reserving a small amount of pasta cooking water.
- Return pasta and vegetables to pot, add olive oil, pesto and cheese.
- Toss lightly to coat, add salt and pepper to taste.
- Add small amount of reserved cooking water if sauce seems too thick.
- Serve immediately.

58. Pasta With Asparagus Lemon Sauce Recipe

Serving: 4 | Prep: | Cook: 20mins | Ready in:

Ingredients

- 1 lb asparagus, tough ends trimmed
- salt
- 1 tsp finely grated lemon zest
- 1/4 c EVOO
- 1 lb penne. mafalde or other pasta
- 1/2 c freshly grated Parmigianno-Reggiano cheese

Direction

- Cut the asparagus into 1 inch pieces, reserve tips separately
- Bring 6 to 8 quarts of water to a boil and add 2 tbsp. salt and cook the asparagus stem until very tender, 6 to 8 minutes
- Transfer with a slotted spoon to a colander, reserving the cooking water in the pot
- Rinse asparagus under cold water and drain well
- Transfer asparagus to a blender or processor
- Cook the asparagus tips in reserved water until just tender, about 3 to 5 minutes
- Transfer tips to a colander, still reserving cooking water
- Rinse under cold water and drain well
- Puree the asparagus stems with the lemon zest, oil and 1/2 C of the asparagus cooking water
- Transfer to a large saucepan
- Cook the pasta according to package directions in the reserved water until not quite al dente, around 3/4s of the cooking time on the package
- Reserve 2 C of the cooking water and drain the pasta
- Add the pasta, asparagus tips and 1/2 C of the reserved water to the asparagus sauce and

cook over medium high, stirring, for 3 to 5 minutes or until pasta is al dente and sauce coats the pasta

- Add more cooking water, 1/4 C at a time, until the sauce coats the pasta but is a little loose (the cheese will thicken it slightly)
- Stir in the cheese and salt and pepper to taste
- Cook, stirring over low until cheese is melted
- Serve immediately

59. Pasta With Pimiento Alfredo Sauce Recipe

Serving: 6 | Prep: | Cook: 20mins | Ready in:

Ingredients

- 12 ounces bow tie pasta
- 3 cups bagged fresh broccoli florets
- 1 can condensed cream of mushroom with roasted garlic soup
- 6-1/2 ounce jar pimientos
- 3/4 cup milk
- 1/3 cup grated parmesan cheese

Direction

- Bring a large pot of water to a boil then add pasta and boil 8 minutes.
- Add broccoli then boil 3 minutes or until pasta and broccoli are firm tender.
- Pour in a colander and drain well then set aside.
- In a blender puree soup, pimientos and milk until smooth.
- Scrape into pasta pot then bring to a boil.
- Remove from heat and add pasta, broccoli and parmesan then toss well to mix.

60. Pasta With Vodka Sauce Recipe

Serving: 6 | Prep: | Cook: 25mins | Ready in:

Ingredients

- 2 teaspoons olive oil, or enough to coat the bottom of your skillet
- 1/2 of a medium sized onion, chopped or diced
- 2 tablespoons water
- 1/4 cup vodka, any brand
- 1 pound dried pasta, penne is my favorite you can use whatever
- 1 can (15 oz) diced tomatoes
- 1 can (8 oz) tomato sauce
- 1/2 teaspoon sugar
- 1/4 teaspoon salt
- 1/4 teaspoon black pepper
- 5 tablespoons grated parmesan cheese, more or less if you like
- 1/2 cup half-and-half
- 1/4 cup fresh basil leaves, shredded (can use a little bit of dried if you don't have fresh)

Direction

- Bring a large pot of salted water to a boil.
- Heat the oil in the skillet over medium-high heat. Add the onion; cook for about 10 minutes, until they are softened, adding the water if needed to prevent any sticking.
- Add the vodka; cook about 3 minutes. Reduce heat to medium.
- Add pasta to the boiling water and cook to al dente, tender yet firm. If you cut into a pasta, like Penne, there shouldn't be a bright white ring in the center, that's a no-no.
- Meanwhile, add tomatoes, tomato sauce, sugar, salt, and pepper to skillet. Cook over medium heat, stirring, 12 minutes.
- Drain pasta and put into a bowl.
- Add parmesan, half-and-half, and basil to the skillet; heat through. Toss with the hot pasta.
- Serve with salad and garlic bread.

61. Pasta And Mussel Sauce Recipe

Serving: 6 | Prep: | Cook: 25mins | Ready in:

Ingredients

- 14 oz shell pasta
- 1 Tbl extra virgin olive oil
- Sauce
- 6 pints mussels, scrubbed
- 1 cup dry white wine
- 1/2 cup butter
- 6 large garlic cloves, chopped fine
- 5 Tbl chopped fresh parsley
- 1 and 1/4 cups heavy cream
- salt and pepper to taste

Direction

- Pull the beards off the mussels and rinse well in several changes of cold water. Discard any mussels that do not close when sharply tapped. Put mussels in large pan with the white wine. Cover pan, shake well, and cook over medium heat for 2-3 minutes until mussels open.
- Remove pan from heat, lift out mussels with slotted spoon, reserving liquid, and set aside until they are cool enough to handle. Discard any mussels that have not opened.
- Melt butter in pan over medium heat, stir in garlic, and cook for 1 minute. Gradually pour in reserved liquid, stirring to blend well. Stir in parsley and cream. Season to taste and bring to a simmer.
- Cook pasta in large pan of boiling salted water, with the oil, for 8-10 minutes, or until tender. Drain pasta, return to pan, cover, and keep warm.
- Remove mussels from shells. Stir mussels into cream sauce. Place pasta in warmed serving dish, pour in the sauce, and toss well to blend. Serve hot, with warm, crusty bread.

62. Pasta With Lemon Cream Sauce Asparagus And Peas Recipe

Serving: 4 | Prep: | Cook: 15mins | Ready in:

Ingredients

- 8 ounces uncooked long fusilli
- 13/4 C (about 1 lb) asparagus cut into 1 1/2" pieces
- 1 C frozen peas, thawed
- 1 Tbl butter
- 1 garlic clove, minced
- 1 C vegetable broth
- 1 tsp cornstarch
- 1/3 C heavy cream
- 3 Tbl fresh lemon juice
- 1/2 tsp salt
- 1/4 tsp pepper
- Dash of cayenne
- Coarsely ground pepper (optional)
- lemon slices(optional)

Direction

- Cook pasta according to package directions, omitting any fat or salt
- Add asparagus during last minute of cooking time
- Place peas in a colander; drain pasta mixture over peas and set aside
- Melt butter in a skillet over medium-high heat
- Add garlic to the pan; sauté 1 minute
- Combine broth and cornstarch in a small bowl; stir until well blended.
- Add broth mixture to pan; bring to a boil
- Cook 1 minute or until thickened, stirring constantly
- Remove from heat
- Stir in cream, juice, salt, the 1/4 tsp. black pepper and the cayenne
- Add pasta mixture to broth mixture; toss gently to coat
- Garnish with coarsely ground black pepper and lemon slices if desired

63. Pasta With Salmon Sauce Recipe

Serving: 4 | Prep: | Cook: 15mins | Ready in:

Ingredients

- 1/4 cup unsalted butter
- 1/2 cup shallots, finely chopped
- 1/2 pound fresh or smoked salmon, thinly sliced
- 2 cups whipping cream
- salt and pepper to taste
- 2 tablespoons Italian flat-leaf parsley, finely chopped
- 1/2 cup parmesan cheese (optional)
- 1 pound linguine or bowtie pasta

Direction

- In a medium sauté pan, melt the butter and cook the shallots for 2-3 minutes.
- Add the salmon and sauté another 2-3 minutes (if you are using smoked salmon, you do not need to cook).
- Add the cream and bring sauce to a boil.
- Remove from heat and add salt and pepper to taste and 1 tablespoon of parsley.
- Keep the sauce warm over low heat.
- In a large pot over high heat, bring water to a boil.
- Cook pasta according to package directions or until al dente.
- Drain the noodles, return them to the cooking pot, and mix in three-quarters of the sauce.
- Transfer to a serving platter and top with remaining sauce, Parmesan cheese and parsley.

64. Pauls Spaghetti Sauce Recipe

Serving: 8 | Prep: | Cook: 120mins | Ready in:

Ingredients

- Sauce
- 2 big cans of tomatoes
- 3 big cans of paste
- 2 ½ cups of water
- 1 tsp savory
- 1 tsp sage
- 1 tsp celery salt
- black pepper
- 1 tablespoon salt
- meatballs
- 3 lbs ground beef
- 1 cup bread crumbs
- Finely chopped onion
- 2 eggs
- 1 cup cheese (shredded)
- salt, pepper
- 1 tsp savory
- 1 tsp sage
- 1 tsp celery salt

Direction

- Place all ingredients for sauce in a large roaster. Then mix all ingredients for the meatballs together and put in sauce raw.
- Put another cup of cheese on top when ready for oven.
- Cover and cook at 350 for 2 hours
- You can add whatever meat you like. I add sausage.

---

65. Penne With Spicy Vodka Tomato Cream Sauce Recipe

Serving: 4 | Prep: | Cook: 25mins | Ready in:

Ingredients

- 1/4 cup extra virgin olive oil
- 3 links sweet Italian sausage
- 4 cloves garlic, minced
- 1/2 - 1 tsp. crushed red pepper flakes (depending on how much heat you like.)
- 1 (28oz) can crushed tomatoes
- 1/2 tsp. salt
- 1 pound penne pasta, cooked and drained
- 1/8 cup vodka
- 1/2 cup heavy whipping cream
- 1/4 cup chopped fresh basil
- 1/3 cup grated parmesan cheese

Direction

- In a large skillet, heat oil over moderate heat. Remove casing from sausage and add the sausage to the skillet. Cook, breaking up the mean until brown. Add garlic and red pepper and cook, stirring until garlic is golden brown. (Be careful not to burn the garlic or it will be bitter!!)
- Add tomatoes and salt, bring to a boil. Reduce heat and simmer for 15 minutes.
- Add vodka, cream and parmesan cheese and bring to a boil. Reduce heat to low and add pasta, toss for 1 minutes. Stir in fresh basil and serve!!

---

66. Pesto And Noodles Recipe

Serving: 4 | Prep: | Cook: 12mins | Ready in:

Ingredients

- 12oz pasta (a penne or elbow is nice because it will capture sauce)
- 1/4 cup pine nuts
- either homemade vegan pesto or store bought (about half a package -- I used Rising Moon Organics Vegan pine nut and basil pesto)
- 1 15oz can of cannellini or great northern or white beans, rinsed and drained
- 1/2 cup frozen peas
- 1/4 cup chiffonaded fresh basil
- 1 tablespoon extra virgin olive oil

Direction

- Cook the pasta according to the instructions on the package. Meanwhile, toast the pine nuts in a fry pan on the stovetop (keep an eye on it though -- it can burn in a flash)

- About 2-3 minutes before the pasta is done, add the frozen peas.
- When the pasta is ready, take out a 1/3 cup of the pasta water and set aside. Drain the pasta and peas, and then place in a large bowl. Add the drained beans, and stir to combine.
- Begin adding the pesto, a spoonful at a time. You want to flavor the pasta, but not overwhelm it with sauce. At the point that the pasta and beans and peas appear lightly covered, taste for seasoning. You may need to add more pesto, salt or pepper. Or if you'd like it a bit saucier, add the pasta water and/or olive oil.
- Garnish with the chiffonade fresh basil and serve immediately!

67. Pesto Recipe

Serving: 8 | Prep: | Cook: | Ready in:

Ingredients

- 1/4 cup pine nuts
- 2 cups fresh basil leaves, picked from the garden
- 2 clove garlic, peeled
- 1/4 cup ounces extra-virgin olive oil
- 1/4 cup freshly grated Parmesan or romano cheese (optional)
- add salt to taste, a few pinches
- 1/2 teaspoon lemon juice

Direction

- In a small skillet brush with olive oil and heat. Add the pine nuts and toast over moderately high heat, stirring constantly, until golden, about 3 minutes.
- Transfer to a plate to cool.
- In a food processor or blender, grind or chop the toasted pine nuts, basil, garlic, and salt until it forms a paste

- Transfer to a high bowl
- Drizzle in the olive oil and lemon juice, beating the mixture all the while with a wooden spoon. If you want an easier method you can slowly add the olive oil and lemon juice into the food processor or blender.
- The pesto can be stored in jars, topped with extra-virgin olive oil, for several weeks.

68. Pesto Sauce Recipe

Serving: 4 | Prep: | Cook: 3mins | Ready in:

Ingredients

- 2 cups fresh basil leaves, packed
- 1/4 cup grated parmesan cheese
- 1/2 cup olive oil
- 3 tablespoons pine nuts or walnuts
- 3 garlic cloves, finely minced

Direction

- Place basil leaves in small batches in food processor and whip until well chopped (do about 3/4 cup at a time).
- Add about 1/3 the nuts and garlic, blend again.
- Add about 1/3 of the Parmesan cheese; blend while slowly adding about 1/3 of the olive oil, stopping to scrape down sides of container.
- Process basil pesto it forms a thick smooth paste.
- Repeat until all ingredients are used, mix all batches together well.
- Serve over pasta.
- Basil pesto keeps in refrigerator one week, or freeze for a few month

69. Pesto Summer Basil In Winter Recipe

Serving: 0 | Prep: | Cook: 1mins |Ready in:

Ingredients

- fresh basil
- Parm cheese, fresh grated, if possible
- roasted garlic, buy it minced, and roasted, if possible. If not roast it.
- pine nuts, get it in bulk section, pan roast 1 min.(Cheap)
- Grated/ peeled lemon rind
- Whole/ Chunk/Kosher/sea salt
- pepper
- EVOO

Direction

- Put basil, and coarse salt/pepper into processor. Process.
- Add toasted nuts, cheese, garlic, lemon rind. Process
- Add desired amt. of EVOO to your liking for serving now, (more) or freezing for later (less). Process.
- You can always add more oil/butter later for desired consistency.
- Varies to your serving needs/ processor size.
- Amounts I use: Basil,1 C packed , 1T Coarse /Whole Salt, a couple pepper grinds, 1/2 tsp. minced roasted garlic, 6-8 passes w/ the grater on the lemon rind, 1/4 C pine nuts, 1/4+ C cheese,1/3-1/2 EVOO. My amounts are based on the size of my processor. Also, the amount of oil is for freezing now purposes. Add more for serving now, or add butter and oil for serving. Same goes for when you thaw and serve later.
- Feel free to experiment. I did.
- Get ice cube trays @ dollar store to freeze in. Then put in freezer bags. You won't mess up your regular ice cube trays, and you can use them next year.

70. Pesto With Walnuts And Pine Nuts Recipe

Serving: 8 | Prep: | Cook: |Ready in:

Ingredients

- 1/2 c. nuts (I use 1/4 walnuts & 1/4 pine nuts)
- 3 T. garlic
- 3 c. fresh basil, spinach, cilantro or combination of greens you like
- 1/2 t. salt
- 1 t. ground pepper
- 1 1/2 c. olive oil
- 1 c. parmeson

Direction

- Combine nuts and garlic in food processor
- Add salt, pepper and greens to food processor & add olive oil until mixture is combined.
- Add parmesan and pulse until smooth.
- Put into containers & coat with a little bit of olive oil.
- Freeze 1/2 & keep 1/2 in fridge.
- Enjoy! It's a winner every time!

71. Pesto Balsamic Penne Pasta Recipe

Serving: 8 | Prep: | Cook: 18mins |Ready in:

Ingredients

- •4 cups bowtie, shell or macaroni pasta, cooked
- •1/2 pound asparagus, diced
- •2.5 oz container of prepared pesto
- 3 carrots, diced
- 1 can drained green beans
- •5 tomatoes, diced or 1 can stewed Italian tomatoes
- •1 tbsp chopped fresh basil

- •2 1/2 Cups of baby spinach leaves
- •4 tbsp balsamic vinegar
- •3 1/2 TBsp Honey-Dijon mustard
- •1/2 tsp dried basil
- •salt and pepper to taste

Direction

- Cook the pasta to your desired softness. I like mine well-cooked and quite soft--18 minutes cook time.
- After it's cooked, drain it and pour the hot pasta into a bowl filled with the spinach leaves and allow the spinach to wilt from the heat of the pasta.
- Then add the can of drained green beans to the bowl and stir.
- Blanch or steam the carrots and asparagus separately in a bit of water just until cooked.
- In a large bowl, combine the asparagus, carrots, pasta and Basil.
- In a small bowl or blender, whisk together the Pesto, Balsamic vinegar, honey-mustard, basil and salt and pepper.
- Pour this dressing over the pasta, stirring well to coat.
- Chill before serving, if desired.

---

72. Pesto Made Easy And Affordable Recipe

Serving: 8 | Prep: | Cook: | Ready in:

Ingredients

- 1-1/2 cups of fresh basil (I can usually grab a package for $2.00 at my local Latino grocery store) - Just rinse really well.
- 3-4 large garlic cloves-minced
- 1/2 cup water-or less (optional is making a less calorie version + 4 tablespoons olive oil)
- 3/4 cup olive oil -or less (I happen to have spanish olive oil which provides a little extra taste similar to that of extra virgin olive oil.)
- 3/4 cup walnuts
- 1/2-3/4 cups freshly grated parmesan cheese (it doesn't have to be parmegiano reggiano which is super expensive - but do not use that stuff from the green can people - oh you know exactly what I am talking about) - And grating it yourself also saves on money. I can usually get a decent brand for $5-6 dollars a good sized wedge that lasts me a month from the cheese section at the large grocery store- and I use slivers of it over salads, and any pasta dishes.
- Kosher or sea salt & freshly cracked pepper
- ***Equipment needed:
- Blender or Food Processor (I have made pesto in both successfully), cutting board, paper towels or clean hand towels

Direction

- This pesto is a creamy pesto which normally does not separate - Adding water also 'extends' the product.
- Also note that mature basil plants (in late August - should you grow your own) will create a more-peppery tasting pesto - versus pesto you may make in May - So in fact you may want to use less of the basil if your leaves are extra big - heck just taste them, put them in your mouth and you will see what I mean. Now take a piece of a little-bitty leaf - tastes different doesn't it? OK, now that, that's out of the way - whew! Back to the directions.
- ***
- Rinsing and washing your basil well, gently shake off any excess water.
- Break or pinch with your fingers (hey get the kids, let them do this work) off any stems and place leaves on paper towels or clean hand towels. Roll them up in paper towels to gently squeeze any extra moisture out of leaves.
- Mince leaves on cutting board as best as you can and place into blender or food processor. (Minced leaves will leave you with about 3/4 cups of basil which is perfect)
- Add your freshly grated cheese, minced garlic, and walnuts to food processor.
- Pulse several times.

- Add half cup of the olive oil and then it's time turn on blender or food processor to max.
- Stop a few times to carefully scrape down any product that may have climbed up the sides.
- Add 1/4 cup or more of olive oil or water. Turn your machine on again, let water get incorporated.
- Now taste-test your pesto - add freshly cracked pepper and salt to your liking.
- Add the rest of the olive oil and/or water should you wish a slightly thinner pesto" And just pulse a few more times to incorporate.
- Pesto lasts for at least 2 weeks in a sealed container in the fridge.
- You can also freeze the pesto too - perfect for those of you who have grown too much basil.
- Let pesto stand out from the fridge for 10 minutes before using to make spreading it easier.
- When adding to pastas, a little goes a long way.
- Enjoy!

73. Piedmontese Sause Recipe

Serving: 4 | Prep: | Cook: 45mins | Ready in:

Ingredients

- 4TBSP Olly Oil
- 8 oz sausage casings removed
- 4 oz good salami chopped
- 2 oz ham chopped
- 1 C chopped Onion
- 6 large garlic thickly sliced
- 1/2 C red wine
- 1 1/2 C beef stock
- 1/2 C heavy cream

Direction

- Sauté sausage in oil, use spoon to break up into small pieces.
- Remove sausage with slotted spoon, reserve and return 3 TBSP of Oil

- Sauté onion and garlic, about 5 minutes, do not burn
- Add meats, stir a minute, add wine, reduce to half, and add stock and cream
- Bring to a boil stirring, reduce to simmer cook for 35 minutes.
- Serve with gnocchi or Pastene fettuccini nests.
- I did not add any cheese.

74. Pumpkin Seed Pesto With Pumpkin Ravioli Recipe

Serving: 8 | Prep: | Cook: 15mins | Ready in:

Ingredients

- 1/2 cup hulled pumpkin seeds (green best)
- 1 1/2 cup packed parsley (fresh)
- 1 small clove garlic
- 1/2 cup EVOO
- 1/2 cup parmesan (fresh, grated)
- 1/4 tsp cayenne pepper
- 1/4 tsp ground cinnamon
- salt
- 2 lbs pumkin ravioli (see other recipe)

Direction

- Bring pot of salted water to a boil. Preheat oven to 350 degrees F. Spread pumpkin seeds on rimmed backing sheet and toast for 5 minutes. Let cool.
- Combine seeds, parsley, and garlic in food processor and process until finely chopped. With motor running, add oil in a steady stream and process until smooth, scraping down sides of bowl as necessary. Scrap mixture into a bowl and stir Parmesan, cayenne, and cinnamon. Season with salt. Pesto will be thick.
- Cook ravioli according to directions. Set aside one cup of pasta cooking water, drain ravioli, and return to pot. Gently stir in pesto and enough reserved water to moisten ravioli. Serve immediately.

75. Quick Meat Sauce Recipe

Serving: 6 | Prep: | Cook: 30mins | Ready in:

Ingredients

- 1 lb. ground beef or poultry
- 1 small onion, chopped
- 2 cloves garlic, minced,
- extra virgin olive oil
- oregano
- a bit of wine
- salt and freshly ground pepper to taste
- 1 quart jar of pasta sauce
- 1/4 cup shredded romano cheese
- 1 pound pasta - cooked per directions, al dente

Direction

- Lightly sauté the onion in some olive oil until turning translucent.
- Add the garlic and just cook briefly, you don't want it brown and bitter.
- Add the chopped meat and keeping sautéing until it is browned, stir often.
- Drain off the fat.
- Stir in oregano, to taste. I use a fairly generous amount, I love it.
- Pour in some wine and stir and scrape the bottom of your pan to deglaze the pan, these bits add flavor.
- Stir in the jar of sauce and then the shredded cheese. Stir until it incorporates.
- Check for seasoning. It's usually fine but you can adjust it with salt and pepper to your taste.
- Mix the sauce into the pasta and serve with grated parmigiana on the side.

76. Quick N Easy Basic Tomatoe Sauce Recipe

Serving: 0 | Prep: | Cook: 15mins | Ready in:

Ingredients

- 3 t olive oil
- 2/3 cup finely chopped onion
- 2 t crushed fresh garlic
- 1 can (28 oz) plum tomatoes, crushed
- 2 t dried basil
- 1 t dried oregano
- 2 bay leaves
- 2 t brown sugar
- Optional: Add ground beef, chicken or soy. Also, to make it thicker, add 2 T of tomatoe paste

Direction

- Heat oil in a large non-stick saucepan over medium heat. Sauté the onion and garlic for 3 mins, stirring often.
- Add tomatoes, basil, oregano, bay leaves and brown sugar. Reduce heat to low and cook for 15 to 20 mins, stirring occasionally until it has reduced slightly.

77. Quick And Easy Pasta Sauce Recipe

Serving: 4 | Prep: | Cook: 7mins | Ready in:

Ingredients

- 40 oz jar of pasta sauce
- 8 squirts of kechtup (for thickness)
- 2 teasoon of lime (or lemon) juice
- 1 tablespoon of hot sauce
- 3 tablespoons of italian thyme
- 1 tablespoon of basil
- sprinkle of garlic powder
- pinch of salt and pepper

Direction

- Put pasta sauce in a sauce pan over high heat on the stove
- Heat until a slow boil
- Turn down heat to a simmer
- Add ketchup, lime juice, and hot sauce
- Stir until mixed in well
- Chop thyme and basil
- Put the herbs in the sauce pan
- Add garlic powder, salt, and pepper
- Stir until mixed in well
- Serve hot over pasta
- Enjoy!

78. Ravioli With Creamy Pesto Sauce Recipe

Serving: 5 | Prep: | Cook: 30mins | Ready in:

Ingredients

- 1 cup whipping cream
- 1 (2.82-ounce) jar pesto sauce
- 2 (9-ounce) packages refrigerated cheese-filled ravioli, uncooked
- 2 tablespoons pine nuts, toasted

Direction

- Combine cream and pesto in a medium saucepan.
- Cook over low heat until thoroughly heated, stirring frequently (do not boil).
- Cook pasta according to package directions in salted water; drain. Toss pasta with whipping cream mixture and sprinkle with pine nuts.
- Serve immediately.

79. Red Pesto Linguine Recipe

Serving: 4 | Prep: | Cook: 20mins | Ready in:

Ingredients

- 8 ounces linguine
- 3 large garlic cloves
- 1-1/2 cups oil packed sundried tomatoes well drained
- 1-1/2 cups chicken broth
- 1 tablespoon extra virgin olive oil
- 1/4 cup chopped fresh Italian parsley
- 1/4 teaspoon salt
- 1/4 teaspoon freshly ground black pepper
- 1/2 cup freshly shredded parmesan cheese

Direction

- Cook linguine according to package directions.
- Meanwhile chop garlic in food processor until finely minced.
- Add tomatoes then process until finely chopped.
- While processor is running slowly add broth and blend until mixture is pureed.
- Heat oil in medium saucepan over medium heat until hot.
- Add tomato mixture and cook 4 minutes or until hot stirring frequently.
- Stir in parsley, salt and pepper then drain linguine and reserve 1/2 cup cooking water.
- Add reserved water to tomato mixture.
- In large bowl toss linguine with tomato mixture then place on serving platter.
- Sprinkle with cheese and serve immediately.

80. Rice Veggie Loaf With Home Made Tomato Sauce Recipe

Serving: 8 | Prep: | Cook: 60mins | Ready in:

Ingredients

- 4 cups of cooked rice, long grain
- 1 can of (sanitarium) mince casserole
- 1/2 red capsicum, diced very small
- 1 stick celery, diced very small
- 1 large onion, chopped small

- 1 medium carrot, grated
- 1 350gram , can of sweet corn kernels
- 2 tsp onion salt
- 1/2 tsp salt (optional)
- 1/2 tsp pepper (optional)
- 1 tbsp oil or butter for fry pan
- Homemade tomatoe sauce (Can be made in advance)
- I Large can diced tomatoe
- 1 tbs tomatoe paste
- 1 tbsp brown vinegar
- 11/2 heaped tbsp sugar
- 1 small granny smith apple grated
- 1 medium onion, grated
- 1 clove of garlic crushed
- 1 tsp salt
- 1/4 tsp pepper

Direction

- You will need large fry pan and an oven dish about, 6-8 cup capacity and 1 small saucepan
- Heat oil in a large fry pan, when hot place, chopped onion, capsicum and celery in pan, lower heat, cook till soft,
- Add grated carrot and cook, through
- Add casserole mince to cooked veggies, mix through
- Sprinkle onion salt, and salt and pepper, mix through well
- Add drained corn kernels, mix through well
- Add the cooked veggie mixture to cooked rice and mix well
- Run a fork down sides of dish, 1 inch apart, little wells for tomato sauce
- Pour tomato sauce over top and spread, so it goes down into where fork punctured
- Place in oven dish
- TO MAKE TOMATOE SAUCE
- Place , tomatoes,, 1/2 of vinegar, sugar, apple, onion, garlic, salt and pepper , in a saucepan and bring to boil, then simmer, taste, to see if tomato mixture requires any more vinegar, keep simmering, till it boils down and thickens, stir to break down tomatoes, About 1 hour

- Place rice dish in 180-200 degree, PRE HEATED oven
- Cook for 1 hour

81. Roasted Grape Tomato Sauce Recipe

Serving: 4 | Prep: | Cook: 20mins | Ready in:

Ingredients

- pint grape tomatoes
- olive oil
- salt
- pepper
- 2 shallots chopped (I've used 1 onion successfully)
- basil
- chives (optional)
- chervil (optional) (I've never used since I can't find)

Direction

- Heat the broiler.
- Put the tomatoes onto a baking sheet, drizzle with 2 tablespoons olive oil, and season with salt and pepper.
- Broil until the tomatoes burst, about 10 minutes.
- In a large skillet over medium-high heat add the remaining 4 tablespoons olive oil.
- Put in the shallots and cook them until they are soft, about 5 minutes.
- Chop the remaining basil, chives, and chervil and add them to the pan.
- Fold the tomatoes into the pan and cook for another 5 minutes.
- Mix into cooked pasta of your choice.

82. Roasted Tomato Marinara Sauce Recipe

Serving: 8 | Prep: | Cook: 90mins |Ready in:

Ingredients

- 3 T. olive oil
- 4 1/2 lbs. tomatoes on the vine (roughly chopped)
- 6 garlic cloves crushed
- 2 T. crushed red pepper
- 4 T. freshly picked basil leaves
- sea salt
- ground black pepper

Direction

- Preheat oven to 400 degrees.
- Throw all ingredient into a roasting pan and toss around to get the olive oil coating everything.
- Roast for about 1 1/2 hours or until the tomatoes have gotten a little color.

83. Roasted Veggie Pasta Sauce Recipe

Serving: 4 | Prep: | Cook: 30mins |Ready in:

Ingredients

- 1 large eggplant
- 1 zucchini
- 1 large onion
- 1 head of garlic
- 2 red, yellow or orange peppers
- 2 roma tomatoes
- olive oil
- salt and pepper
- rosemary
- basil
- chili flakes if desired

Direction

- Chop up all veggies into equal sized pieces.
- Place on cookie sheet and drizzle with olive oil, making sure veggies are coated.
- Season with salt and pepper, a sprinkle of rosemary and basil.
- Roast in oven at 400 degrees for 30 minutes or until veggies are soft and caramelized.
- Put roasted veggies in food processor and whiz up. Add chili flakes here if you like a bit of kick!
- Serve over warm pasta or with pita bread as a dip.

84. Rocket Pesto Recipe

Serving: 8 | Prep: | Cook: 5mins |Ready in:

Ingredients

- 2 bunches arugula, rinsed and roughly chopped
- juice and zest of 1 lemon
- kosher salt and fresh black pepper to taste
- About 1/4 cup good olive oil

Direction

- Optional: blanch arugula briefly in boiling water; this will help preserve its bright green color and soften it up a little for the blending step.
- Add arugula, lemon juice and zest, salt and pepper to blender or food processor.
- Blend, drizzling olive oil slowly until mixture has become a smooth paste.
- Store in fridge, or freeze in ice-cube tray for individual size servings.

85. SLOW COOKER VEGETABLE PASTA SAUCE Recipe

Serving: 6 | Prep: | Cook: 430mins | Ready in:

Ingredients

- One 14.5 ounce can diced tomatoes (DO NOT DRAIN)
- one 6 ounce can tomato paste
- 1-1/2 cups sliced, fresh mushrooms
- 1 medium red pepper, chopped
- 1 medium green pepper, chopped
- 1 small zucchini, cut into 1/4 inch slices
- 2 green onions, green and white parts sliced
- 1 Tablespoon dried chopped parsley
- oregano, to taste
- basil, to taste
- minced garlic, to taste
- Hot, cooked fettuccini or linguine noodles

Direction

- Spray a 3.5-quart crockpot with no-stick cooking spray. Place all of the ingredients EXCEPT cooked pasta in crockpot and stir thoroughly. Cover and cook on LOW setting 7-8 hours. Serve over hot, cooked pasta. Top with shredded Parmesan cheese, if desired.
- Note: I always cut up the vegetables the night before and put them altogether in a covered Tupperware container. Then the next day all I have to do is mix everything together in the crockpot, give it a good stir, and go!

86. SPAGHETTI SAUCE THREE WAYS Recipe

Serving: 4 | Prep: | Cook: 60mins | Ready in:

Ingredients

- Plain Marinara Sauce:
- 1 Tablespoon olive oil
- about 1/2 cup chopped onion
- one 14.5 ounce can diced tomatoes (DO NOT DRAIN)
- one 8 ounce can tomato sauce
- one 6 ounce can tomato paste
- 1/2 cup or so water
- dried oregano, to taste
- minced garlic, to taste
- minced fresh or dried basil, to taste
- minced fresh or dried parsley, to taste
- 1 teaspoon sugar (to cut the acid in the tomatoes)
- .
- .
- Meatballs:
- 1/3 pound ground sirloin
- 1/3 pound ground pork
- 1/4 cup finely chopped onion
- 1/3-1/2 cup quick oats
- 1 egg
- minced garlic, to taste
- minced fresh or dried parsley, to taste
- minced fresh or dried basil, to taste
- salt and pepper, to taste
- .
- .
- Meat-Based Sauce:
- 1 pound ground sirloin or italian sausage (or a combination of both)

Direction

- Plain Marinara Sauce:
- In a large pot, brown onion in olive oil until tender and "clear", but not brown. Stir in remaining ingredients and simmer 30 minutes, stirring occasionally. If making meatballs, make them while the sauce is simmering. If serving the sauce as is, simmer an hour.
- Meatballs:
- Heat oven to 350 degrees. In a medium bowl, combine all of the meatball ingredients (I use my hands to blend them together better). Shape mixture into balls 1-1/2 inches in diameter (again, I don't measure, but that is about how big they look to me). Place meatballs on a parchment paper lined baking

sheet. Bake about 15 minutes, until lightly browned on the bottoms. Drain on paper towels to remove any grease. Gently stir meatballs into sauce and simmer 30 minutes, stirring occasionally.

- Meat-Based Sauce:
- Brown meat and onions together in a large pot. After I brown the meat and onions, I put them in a colander and rinse them with cold water to remove any grease. Return them to the pot and add the remaining ingredients from the marinara sauce. If the sauce looks a little pale in color, add a little sweet Hungarian paprika (I use Penzeys). It doesn't really add flavor, but makes the sauce a deep, rich, red color. Simmer, stirring occasionally, about an hour.
- Serve any of the versions over hot, cooked pasta (we like linguine or fettuccini better than regular spaghetti noodles) and top with shredded Parmesan cheese. Add a salad and garlic bread, and you have an Italian meal that is better than anything from a jar! Oh, and any leftovers freeze beautifully.

87. SUN DRIED TOMATO PESTO WITH BOWTIE PASTA Recipe

Serving: 12 | Prep: | Cook: 30mins | Ready in:

Ingredients

- 1 L>b. uncooked bow tie pasta
- 1{8 oz. Jar sundriend tomatoes in olive oil
- 8 Oz.s. peppered bacon
- 1 {10 0z. Jar basil pesto
- 1 cup grated romano cheese
- Coarsley ground black pepper

Direction

- Cook pasta according to directions drain tomatoes reserve some of the oil cut tomatoes into thin strips

- Cook Bacon in skillet until crisp
- Drain and Crumble
- Drain Pasta and place in large bowl Add tomatoes and pesto mix well add Bacon and cheese toss well
- For moister consistency add some of reserved sun dried tomato oil Season with black pepper.
- Found in newspaper

88. Salami And Tomato Sauce Recipe

Serving: 2 | Prep: | Cook: 20mins | Ready in:

Ingredients

- 1/2 lb salami, cut in strips
- 1 16 oz can tomato puree
- 1 medium onion, sliced
- 2 cloves garlic, sliced
- 1 Tbsp olive oil
- salt and pepper to taste

Direction

- Heat a frying pan over medium heat until hot.
- Add olive oil. When hot add onions and garlic and cook until tender (try not to brown, it changes the flavor).
- Add salami and cook about 2 minutes, then add the tomatoes, salt and pepper. Bring to a boil, then lower heat and simmer uncovered 20 minutes or until it is as thick as you like.
- Serve over your favorite pasta with lots of parmesan cheese.

89. Scallops And Pasta With Pistachio Parsley Pesto Recipe

Serving: 2 | Prep: | Cook: 15mins | Ready in:

Ingredients

- 1 cup chopped fresh parsley
- 3 Tbsp coarslely chopped pistachios
- 1 tsp grated lemon rind
- 1/4 tsp ground cumin
- 1/4 tsp pepper
- 1/8 tsp salt
- 1/8 tsp paprika
- 2 Tbsp fresh lemon juice
- 1 1/4 tsp olive oil
- 3/4 pound sea scallops
- 1/4 cup all-purpose flour
- 1/8 tsp salt
- 2 tsp margarine
- 2 cups cooked angel hair (about 4 ounces uncooked pasta)
- Freshley groound pepper
- parsley sprigs (optional)

Direction

- Place first 9 ingredients in a food processor; process until smooth, scraping sides of processor bowl occasionally.
- Combine scallops, flour, and 1/4 tsp. salt in large zip-top plastic bag; seal and shake to coat.
- Heat margarine in non-stick skillet over medium-high heat. Add scallops; cook 3 1/2 minutes on each side or until scallops are done.
- Combine pesto mixture and pasta in a large bowl, tossing well. Arrange 1 cup pasta on each plate, and divide scallops evenly between plates. Sprinkle with pepper; garnish with parsley, if desired.

90. Seafood Variations Of Sugo Alla Carrettiera Tomato And Basil Sauce Recipe

Serving: 6 | Prep: | Cook: 30mins | Ready in:

Ingredients

- Prepared sauce from Sugo Alla Carrettiera recipe
- 1 1/2 cups gamberi (shrimps) or cozze (mussels) or aragosta (lobster)
- 2 tbsp Italian parsley
- 1/4 cup dry white wine
- pasta choice: spaghetti

Direction

- The preparation is the same with the addition of 1/4 cup dry white wine to step 2 with the parsley.
- The mussels, shrimps or lobster pieces are added to the tomato sauce at the very end of the simmering period.
- Again, red pepper flakes are used in this sauce with amount varying to one's taste of spiciness.
- Top with freshly grated formaggio Parmigiano-Reggiano.
- Bon Appetit!

91. Sicilian Spaghetti Sauce Recipe

Serving: 6 | Prep: | Cook: 2mins | Ready in:

Ingredients

- Ingredients
- 1/2 pound mild Italian sausage
- 1/2 pound lean ground beef
- 1 large onion, chopped
- 2 cloves garlic, minced
- 4 (8-ounce) cans tomato sauce
- 1 (6-ounce) can Italian-style tomato paste
- 3 cups water
- 1/4 cup sugar
- 1 to 1 1/2 teaspoons salt
- 1 teaspoon dried parsley
- 1 teaspoon dried basil
- 1/4 to 1/2 teaspoon ground red pepper
- 1 cup sliced fresh mushrooms

- Hot cooked linguine
- Shredded parmesan cheese

Direction

- Preparation
- Remove casings from sausage, and discard. Cook sausage and ground beef in a large skillet or Dutch oven over medium heat 6 minutes, stirring until meat crumbles. Add onion and garlic, and sauté 4 minutes or until beef and sausage are no longer pink. Drain and set aside. Wipe skillet clean.
- Combine sauce and next 7 ingredients in skillet or Dutch oven; cook, stirring occasionally, 1 hour. Add sausage mixture and mushrooms. Cook, stirring occasionally, 1 hour and 30 minutes or until mixture thickens. Serve over linguine; sprinkle with cheese. Serve with breadsticks, if desired.

92. Simple Tomato Sauce Recipe

Serving: 1 | Prep: | Cook: 15mins | Ready in:

Ingredients

- 2 fair sized tomatoes, finely chopped with core and seeds removed
- 2 tablespoons of olive oil or normal oil
- 1 tablespoon of crushed or finely chopped garlic
- 1 teaspoon of ketchup
- 3 tablespoons of sweetcorn [optional]
- 2 tablespoons of finely chopped pepper [optional]
- tabasco/chilli [optional]
- black pepper
- salt

Direction

- Heat up the olive oil in a saucepan
- Then throw in the garlic
- Now stir it for 7 seconds

- Throw in the finely chopped tomato and stir
- Using a potato masher, mash up the tomatoes while being cooked
- Stir and cook the tomatoes until it becomes thick
- Stir in the ketchup
- Now add in tabasco or chilli [optional]
- Now add in the sweetcorn or finely chopped pepper [optional]
- Add the black pepper and stir
- Now add salt to taste
- Add the sauce to pasta or your chosen dish

93. Simplicty Tomato Sauce Recipe

Serving: 4 | Prep: | Cook: 45mins | Ready in:

Ingredients

- 1 large can Italian plum tomatoes
- 5 tablespoons butter
- 1 small onion, peeled and cut in half
- 1T salt
- pasta
- Parmagianno-Reggiano cheese, grated

Direction

- Put the tomatoes in a saucepan and with very clean kitchen scissors cut them up. Add the butter, onion and salt and bring to a light simmer.
- Cook uncovered for 45 minutes or until the fat floats from the tomato. Stir occasionally, using a wooden spoon to mash any large piece of tomato. Taste and correct for salt. Discard onion and toss sauce with pasta. Serve with grated cheese.

94. Skillet Garden Tomato Sauce Recipe

Serving: 8 | Prep: | Cook: 30mins | Ready in:

Ingredients

- 20 - 30 ripe tomatoes, cored
- 1/4 cup Ex virgin olive oil
- 6 cloves of garlic sent through a rasp
- 1 lg. onion minced
- 1/2 cup of red wine
- 1/4 cup minced flat leaf parsley
- 1 tsp red pepper flakes
- salt, pepper, sugar if need to rid the acidity

Direction

- Core all the tomatoes
- Place in a kettle with boiling salted water
- Remove the tomatoes from the pot when the skins start to slip off; drain
- In a very large skillet put the olive oil and heat on med until a drop of water "bounces" when dropped in.
- Add the onion and sauté for 5 minutes
- Add the garlic and sauté for 1 minute
- Set aside
- Remove the skins from the tomatoes
- Put in a food processor and pulsate in batches until you obtain the consistency that you like
- Pour into the skillet
- Add some wine
- Add the parsley, salt and pepper
- Simmer for 30 minutes, uncovered,
- Place a ladle full of the sauce in a small bowl, allow to cool slightly and taste,
- Adjust the flavorings
- Now you have a basic tomato sauce that you can add meats, cheeses and vegetables to
- I like it just like this with a loaf of fresh Italian bread and a bowl of olive oil and minced garlic and a bottle of Red Table Wine. Now that's living!!!

95. Slognese Sauce (Slow Cooked Bolognese Style Sauce) Recipe

Serving: 6 | Prep: | Cook: 5hours | Ready in:

Ingredients

- 2lbs finely ground or minced beef, venison, veal, lamb or any combo of the above*
- ~15oz crushed tomoatoes
- ~24oz tomato sauce
- 1 medium onion, grated(I left about 1/4 of the onion in larger pieces, but that's not needed)
- 1 large carrot, grated(I used a handful of baby carrots, as the only whole carrots I use at all are in a cooler in my barn for the horses ;-)
- 2 stalks celery, sliced thin
- 3 cloves garlic, minced
- several dashes of hickory liquid smoke
- 1 cup dry wine(I used a Sauvignon Blanc)
- 1-1 1/2 cups half and half(can sub heavy cream, if desired)
- kosher or sea salt and fresh ground pepper

Direction

- Add all ingredients, except for the half and half, to slow cooker.
- Stir well.
- Heat on low for about 3-4 hours, until meat is cooked through. It's okay to stir this every hour or so. If your pot runs really hot, stir even more often. Don't let a bunch of this stick to the sides.
- Remove lid and let cook another 1-2 hours, also stirring every 30 minutes or so to thicken nicely.
- Add half and half about 30 minutes before ready to serve, and let warm on warm or low setting, without lid. (If using cream, you might not have to let it cook at all, any more, as it might be thick enough :)
- Taste and add more salt and pepper, if needed.
- Serve over pasta. I used whole grain penne and added just a touch of fresh grated Parmesan for contrast, more than flavor

- And, this screamed for garlic bread!
- *make sure your ground meat is finely ground. If it's got the wavy, longer texture of some market packaged meats, it's not fine enough. If tossing it in a grinder isn't an option, just use two large knives and hand mince it!

96. Smoky Pumpkin Marinara With Andoullie Recipe

Serving: 6 | Prep: | Cook: 2hours | Ready in:

Ingredients

- 1lb Andoullie sausage links, sliced
- olive oil
- 1 onion, finely diced
- 3 cloves garlic, minced
- 1 roasted red pepper, diced
- 2 cups tomato sauce
- 2 cups crushed tomatoes
- 1 cup pumpkin puree
- 1-4 chipotle peppers, minced
- 1-3T adobo sauce from the chipotles
- 1T fresh oregano, minced(or sub 1t dried)
- 1T fresh basil, minced(or sub 1t dried)
- couple splashes of liquid smoke
- 1T smoked paprika
- 2T butter
- Kosher or sea salt and plenty of fresh ground pepper

Direction

- Heat oil over medium heat.
- Add onion and sausage and cook a few minutes until onions begin to soften.
- Add garlic and red pepper and cook another 2 minutes or so.
- Add remaining ingredients up through butter.
- Simmer, stirring occasionally, for at least 30 minutes, but longer is better, so at least an hour, if possible.

- Add salt and pepper as needed
- Add butter, stirring until melted and serve over pasta :)

97. Spaghetti Sauce In Bulk Recipe

Serving: 10 | Prep: | Cook: 480mins | Ready in:

Ingredients

- 2 jars of your favorite store spaghetti sauce
- 2-14.5 oz cans peeled and diced tomatoes
- 2-14.5 oz. cans of stewed tomatoes
- 12oz. tomato paste
- 2 onions chopped
- 4-6 cloves garlic-minced
- 2 tsp. dried thyme
- 2 Tbsp. dried oregano
- 2 Tbsp. dried basil
- 2 bay leaves
- 1 1/2 lb. mild italian sausage ring
- 1 lb. either ground beef or meatballs(see my meatball recipe that is what we use)
- 2 tsp. olive oil

Direction

- In a frying pan brown ground beef if using, drain and place in crockpot. If using meatballs just add 'em (I don't even thaw them)
- Brown the sausage in olive oil on each side not cooked through just browned.
- Remove and place in crockpot.
- Add onions and garlic to oil and sauté' until glassy and add to crockpot. (Careful not to brown garlic will be yucky if it gets brown)
- Dump everything else in.
- Give it a stir and cook on low for 6-8 hours.
- Eat some for dinner and pack the rest away in the freezer for the rest of the week!! If you feel like it go ahead and throw a lasagna together and freeze for a quick dinner. (I freeze the sausage by itself for sausage sandwiches so on dinner day just sauté some onions and green peppers!)

98. Spaghetti Sauce Recipe

Serving: 5 | Prep: | Cook: 190mins | Ready in:

Ingredients

- 1 2 lb. can tomatoes
- 1 small onion, cut in eighths
- 1/2 green bell pepper, cut in 1" pieces
- 1 clove garlic
- 1 Tbsp. brown sugar
- 2 Tbsp. white vinegar
- 1 tsp. salt
- 1/4 tsp. black pepper
- 1 tsp. oregano
- 2 bay leaves
- 1 8 oz. can tomato sauce
- 7 oz. Traditional flavor Ragu sauce
- 1 & 1/2 lbs. mild Italian sausage
- cooked spaghetti
- grated parmesan cheese

Direction

- Put first nine ingredients into blender container.
- Cover and process for two cycles.
- Pour into large sauce pan.
- Add bay leaves, tomato sauce and Ragu.
- Heat to boiling, reduce heat and simmer 30 minutes, semi covered.
- While the sauce is simmering, brown the sausage in a large frying pan.
- Cut the sausage into bite size pieces and add to sauce.
- Simmer for one hour, semi covered.
- Remove bay leaves.
- Serve over spaghetti with parmesan cheese.

99. Spaghetti With Arugula Pesto And Seared Jumbo Shrimp Recipe

Serving: 6 | Prep: | Cook: 15mins | Ready in:

Ingredients

- 2 cups fresh arugula
- 1 garlic clove
- 1/2 cup plus 2 tablespoons olive oil
- 1/2 cup freshly grated Parmesan
- salt and freshly ground black pepper
- 1 pound jumbo shrimp
- 1 pound spaghetti
- lemon zest, for garnish
- 10 parsley leaves, chopped, for garnish

Direction

- Blend the arugula and garlic in a food processor until finely chopped. With the machine running, gradually add 1/2 cup of oil, processing until well blended. Transfer the pesto to a large bowl. Stir in the Parmesan. Season with salt and pepper, to taste.
- Prepare the grill (high heat). Using a knife, cut the back of the shrimp. Brush the shrimp with oil. Sprinkle with salt. Grill the shrimp until just cooked through, about 3 minutes per side. Transfer the shrimp to a plate.
- Meanwhile, cook the pasta in a large pot of boiling salted water until tender but still firm to the bite, stirring occasionally, about 8 minutes. Drain, reserving 1/2 cup of the cooking liquid.
- Toss the pasta with the pesto in the large bowl to coat, adding the reserved cooking liquid 1 tablespoon at a time to moisten. Top with the grilled shrimp. Garnish with the lemon zest and parsley.

100. Spaghetti With Olive Oil, Garlic, Chili And Lemon Recipe

Serving: 4 | Prep: | Cook: 20mins |Ready in:

Ingredients

- - ⅛ cup extra-virgin olive oil
- - ¼ cup thinly sliced garlic (about 6 to 8 cloves)
- - ½ tsp red pepper flakes
- - Juice of ½ lemon
- - 3 tbsp finely chopped flat-leaf parsley
- - ½ cup grated Parmesan cheese
- - 1 pound spaghetti

Direction

- - Cook spaghetti according to package directions until al dente.
- - Meanwhile, in a large skillet set over medium-high heat, heat olive oil. - Add garlic and red pepper flakes and cook until garlic is golden, about 3 minutes, stirring constantly.
- - Remove from heat and stir in lemon juice.
- - Drain pasta, then add to skillet. Toss well to combine.
- - Serve immediately, sprinkled with parsley and Parmesan.

101. Spaghetti With Olive Sauce Recipe

Serving: 4 | Prep: | Cook: 20mins |Ready in:

Ingredients

- 1 cup sliced assorted pitted olives
- 1 (26 ounce) jar favorite spaghetti sauce
- 1 (8 ounce) package spaghetti
- grated parmesan cheese

Direction

- Cook spaghetti according to package directions.
- Meanwhile, simmer spaghetti sauce and olives until heated through.
- Drain spaghetti.
- To serve, put spaghetti on plates and top with desired amount of sauce.
- Top with Parmesan cheese.

102. Spaghetti With Onion Sauce Recipe

Serving: 4 | Prep: | Cook: 30mins |Ready in:

Ingredients

- 2 medium white onions
- 1/4 cup extra virgin olive oil
- 1 teaspoon salt
- 2 tablespoons hot water
- 2 teaspoons freshly ground black pepper
- 4 anchovy fillets chopped
- 1 pound spaghetti
- 1/4 cup grated parmesan cheese

Direction

- Slice onions very thin.
- Heat half of the olive oil in a large saucepan.
- Add onions, water, salt and pepper then cook over low heat covered 15 minutes.
- Add anchovies and cook another 5 minutes.
- Add remaining olive oil then remove from heat and keep warm.
- Bring 4 quarts of water to a boil then add 1 tablespoon salt and cook spaghetti al dente.
- Drain and put into a warmed serving bowl then dress with onion sauce tossing well.
- Serve with grated parmesan cheese.

103. Spaghetti With Texas Style Sauce Recipe

Serving: 4 | Prep: | Cook: 20mins |Ready in:

Ingredients

- 1 box spaghetti
- 1 can stewed tomatoes
- 3 medium onions
- 8 strips bacon
- 1 tablespoon chili powder
- 1 clove garlic
- 1/2 pound grated American cheese

Direction

- Chop bacon into fine pieces and fry until quite crisp.
- Put in finely chopped onions and garlic then fry until quite brown.
- Drain off half the juice from the tomatoes then add them and remaining juice to sauce.
- Add chili powder, salt and pepper then boil spaghetti in salted water until soft.
- Butter a large platter and spread half of the spaghetti evenly on it.
- Cover this with half of the sauce and half of the grated cheese.
- Repeat with layers of the remaining spaghetti, sauce and cheese.
- Place platter in a warm oven and melt the cheese then serve.

---

104. Spaghetti With Walnut Sage Pesto Recipe

Serving: 4 | Prep: | Cook: 25mins | Ready in:

Ingredients

- 1 lb dried spaghetti
- 1/3 cup chopped fresh parsley
- 3 to 4 tablespoons chopped fresh sage
- 1 garlic clove, chopped
- 1 teaspoon salt
- 1/2 to 1 cup walnuts, toasted and cooled (toast nuts in a shallow baking pan in a 350° F oven until golden, 5 to 15 minutes)
- 1/3 cup olive oil

- 1/3 cup grated parmigiano-Reggiano plus additional for serving
- 1/4 teaspoon black pepper

Direction

- Cook spaghetti in a 6-quart pot of boiling salted water until al dente.
- While pasta is boiling, blend parsley, sage, and garlic with salt in a food processor until finely chopped.
- Add walnuts and pulse until finely chopped.
- With motor running, add oil in a steady stream.
- Turn off motor, then add 1/3 cup cheese and pepper and pulse to combine.
- Reserve 1 cup cooking water, then drain pasta in a colander.
- Thin pesto with reserved cooking water in a serving bowl, then add pasta and toss to combine.
- Sprinkle with cheese before serving.

---

105. Spicy Sausage Red Pasta Sauce Recipe

Serving: 6 | Prep: | Cook: 90mins | Ready in:

Ingredients

- 2 hot Italian sausages (8 ounces), casings removed
- 1 cup finely chopped onion
- 1 (or more to taste) large garlic clove, peeled and finely minced
- 1/2 teaspoon fennel seed
- Pinch of cayenne (or more to taste)
- 1 teaspoon sea salt
- 1/4 cup extra virgin olive oil
- 4 cups tomato juice (lower salt varieties are much better for this - I use a Knudsen organic juice)
- 1 pound dried pasta (shells, rigatoni or spaghetti)
- 1 cup fresh ground parmigiano-Reggiano

Direction

- Crumble sausage meat and combine well with onions, garlic and fennel seed in a bowl with 1 1/2 cups cold water. Cover and refrigerate for at least 30 minutes or up to several hours.
- Transfer the sausage mixture to a large, heavy-bottomed saucepan with a lid. Stir in the cayenne (add more if you want it spicy) and salt, and pour over the olive oil. Bring to a boil and cook, stirring often, over moderate heat until all the water has cooked away and only the oil remains to moisten the ingredients.
- Add the tomato juice, cover, and bring to a boil. Reduce heat and gently simmer for 30 minutes with the lid slightly ajar.
- While the sauce simmers, bring a large pot of water to a boil. Generously salt the water and add the pasta. Cook until al dente.
- Drain the pasta and transfer to a heated serving bowl. Ladle enough sauce to generously coat the pasta with a little puddle on the bottom. Sprinkle over the Parmigiano-Reggiano and toss. The cheese will thicken the sauce. If it seems dry, add more sauce.
- Serve right away with extra sauce and cheese passed at the table.

---

106.   Spinach And Ricotta Pesto Recipe

Serving: 6 | Prep: | Cook: | Ready in:

Ingredients

- spinach and Ricotta Pesto
- 2 tablespoons walnuts
- 1/2 pound spinach washed and trimmed
- 1 small clove garlic coarsely chopped
- 2 tablespoons olive oil
- 1/2 cup ricotta cheese
- 1/4 cup grated parmesan cheese
- 1/2 teaspoon salt
- 1/2 teaspoon freshly ground black pepper

Direction

- Place walnuts, spinach and garlic in work bowl of a food processor.
- Process until finely chopped scraping sides of bowl as necessary.
- With motor running pour in olive oil until a smooth paste forms.
- Scrape mixture into a medium bowl and stir in ricotta, parmesan, salt and pepper.

---

107.   Sugo Alla Carrettiera Tomato And Basil Sauce Recipe

Serving: 5 | Prep: | Cook: 40mins | Ready in:

Ingredients

- 3/4 cup extra virgin olive oil
- 8 large cloves garlic, peeled and sliced thinly
- 2 lbs. fresh ripe plum tomatoes, peeled, seeded and coursely chopped (or 3 cups canned Italian plum tomatoes)
- 1 1/2 cups fresh basil leaves, torn by hand into pieces
- 1/2 tsp salt
- Freshly grated formaggio parmigiano-reggiano (serve separately)
- Pinch of pepperoncini (red pepper flakes) - optional
- pasta choice: spaghetti, spaghettini, penne, Rigatoni

Direction

- Put all but 1 tsp. of olive oil and garlic in a large skillet over medium-heat and cook until the garlic begins to sizzle.
- Add the torn basil leaves and cook for three minutes. Remove the leaves and set aside.
- Add the tomatoes as soon as the garlic begins to change color. If using fresh tomatoes, you'll notice that they will give off a fair amount of liquid. When the liquid begins to reduce,

season with salt. If using canned tomatoes, season with salt at the beginning.

- Continue cooking over medium-heat until tomatoes have reduced and separated from the oil. At this point, you have the option to add the pepperoncini.
- Add basil leaves. Reduce heat and let simmer for another 30 minutes.
- Cook al dente your pasta of choice. Drain pasta and toss with the sauce in the skillet, adding remaining tbsp. of olive oil.
- Serve individual portions of pasta with sauce. Top with grated formaggio Parmigiano-Reggiano.
- Bon appetit!

108.   Sundried Tomato And Basil Pesto Recipe

Serving: 4 | Prep: | Cook: 5mins | Ready in:

Ingredients

- 1 cup of sundried tomatoes, roughly chopped (not oil packed)
- 1 cup of fresh basil leaves, roughly chopped
- 3-4 cloves of garlic, minced
- Zest of one lemon
- juice of half a lemon
- 1/2 cup grated parmesan cheese
- salt and pepper
- olive oil

Direction

- Put all ingredients except olive oil in food processor and pulse 15 times until well incorporated.
- Turn on food processor and stream in olive oil until desired consistency - not too wet, not too dry.

109.   Sunflower Seed And Cilantro Pesto Recipe

Serving: 8 | Prep: | Cook: | Ready in:

Ingredients

- 1/2 c sunflower seeds-hulled, roasted, unsalted
- 1 bunch cilantro-washed and chopped
- 3 cloves garlic-peeled
- 1/2 tsp dried chipotle optional
- 1/4 c olive oil

Direction

- Blend first 4 ingredients in a processor or blender until it becomes a paste.
- Add olive oil slowly while processing,
- Blend until it is incorporated.

110.   Tomato And Garlic Sauce Recipe

Serving: 46 | Prep: | Cook: 60mins | Ready in:

Ingredients

- 3 T. olive oil
- 1 c. finely chopped onions
- 1 T. finely chopped garlic
- 4 c. peeled and seeded roma tomatoes or Italian whole pack tomatoes (chopped but not drained)
- 1-6 oz. can tomato paste
- 1 T. dried oregano crumbled
- 1 T. finely cut fresh basil or 1 t. dried basil, crumbled
- 1 bay leaf
- 2 t. sugar
- 1 1/2 t. salt
- freshly ground black pepper

Direction

- In a 3-4 quart stainless-steel saucepan, heat the 3 tablespoons of olive oil and cook the finely chopped onions in it over medium heat, stirring frequently, for 7-8 minutes. When the onions are soft and transparent but are not brown, add the tablespoon of finely chopped garlic and cook for another 1-2 minutes, stirring constantly. Then stir in the coarsely chopped tomatoes and their liquid, the tomato paste, oregano, basil, bay leaf, sugar, salt and a few grindings of black pepper. Bring the sauce to a boil, turn the heat to very low and simmer uncovered, stirring occasionally, for about 1 hour.
- When finished, the sauce should be thick and fairly smooth. Remove the bay leaf. Taste and season the sauce with salt and freshly ground black pepper. If you wish a smoother texture, puree the sauce through a food mill, I use my stick blender.

---

111.   Tomato Sauce Alla Napolitana Recipe

Serving: 2 | Prep: | Cook: 10mins | Ready in:

Ingredients

- 2 cups tomato puree
- 1/4 cup olive oil
- 4 garlic cloves
- 1 chili pepper (pepperoncini)
- 1/4 cup of fresh basil leaves
- salt and pepper

Direction

- Crush and peel the garlic.
- Heat a pan and add the olive oil. When hot add the chili pepper. Cook until it takes some color. Add the garlic and cook until golden (NOT brown or it will be bitter). Remove the garlic and pepper. The garlic and pepper should flavor the oil, but not be in the finished sauce.

- Add the tomato puree, bring to the boil. Reduce heat to medium and let reduce until it is as thick as you like. (For me this was about 10 minutes.)
- Add some salt and pepper.
- Add the basil leaves and add your favorite pasta to the pan. Mix and serve.

---

112.   Tomato Sauce In The Oven Recipe

Serving: 10 | Prep: | Cook: 40mins | Ready in:

Ingredients

- 1 kg ripe tomatoes cut in chunks.
- 2 big onions roughly chopped.
- 4 cloves garlic roughly chopped.
- 1 tbs oregano leaves .
- 1 tbs thyme leaves.
- 1 tbs rosemary leaves.
- 4 basilicum leaves.
- olive oil.
- cayenne pepper or tabasco or chilli (optionnal).
- salt.
- pepper from the mill to taste.
- 1 tbs balsamico vinegar.

Direction

- Chop the aromatic herbs.
- Preheat oven to 200 C.
- Put 1 tbsp. olive oil in the oven tray and divide with a brush or you hand.
- Put tomato chunks in tray, top with onion, garlic and herbs, add salt and pepper to taste, add balsamic and 2 tbsp. olive oil, mix well.
- Bake in oven 40 min, stir twice.
- Take out and let cool.
- Mix in the blender till you have a smooth sauce, taste again with salt and pepper.
- If you like it hot then add 1 tsp. tabasco or 1 tsp. cayenne pepper or ground chili.

- Using parsley, celery, mustard or lemon juice will give you also a tasty tomato sauce, use your phantasy.

113. Tomato Sauce Recipe

Serving: 4 | Prep: | Cook: 90mins | Ready in:

Ingredients

- 1 Tin of chopped tomatoes
- 6 cloves of garlic
- 2 shallots
- 1 Cup of extra virgin greek olive oil
- 1 teaspoon of chopped basil
- 1 Table spoon of Pernod
- 1 Bunch of thyme
- 1 Small bunch of oregano
- 1/2 a baie leave
- 1 Soup spoon of caster sugar
- salt and pepper

Direction

- Finely chop the garlic (don't forget to take the centre off) and the shallots.
- Sweat off the herbs, the garlic and the chopped shallots with half of the olive oil for 8 minutes.
- Add the tomatoes, the sugar the rest of the olive oil.
- Gently simmer for 1h30.
- Season well and remove the thyme and the bay leaf.
- It is ready!
- Note that you can replace all the fresh herbs with a table spoon of dried mixed herbs.

114. Tomato Vodka Cream Sauce Supreme Recipe

Serving: 6 | Prep: | Cook: 120mins | Ready in:

Ingredients

- 1/2 cup butter
- 1/2 teaspoon crushed red pepper flakes
- 1/2 cup vodka
- 1 large can Italian crushed tomatoes
- 1 cup heavy cream
- 1/2 cup grated romano cheese
- 1/2 cup grated parmesan cheese
- 1 pound mild Italian sausage
- 1 green pepper, chopped
- 1 large onion, chopped
- 1 cup sliced fresh mushrooms
- 2 cloves garlic, minced
- 1 small eggplant, peeled and diced
- 2 large tomatoes, chopped
- salt and pepper to taste
- 1 tablespoon hot pepper sauce
- 1/4 cup chopped fresh parsley

Direction

- In large pan, melt the butter until bubbly. Add crushed red pepper flakes and Italian tomatoes. Bring to a simmer. Add vodka. Let simmer for about 5 minutes. Add cheeses, let melt.
- Add heavy cream. Turn to low and cover.
- Meanwhile in skillet, brown mushrooms in 1 tablespoon olive oil. Add green pepper, onion and garlic. Sauté for about 5 minutes until soft. Add to the vodka sauce mixture. Brown Italian sausage and add to vodka sauce mixture.
- Add diced eggplant and tomatoes to the vodka mixture along with hot sauce. Add salt and pepper to taste. Let simmer on low heat for roughly 60 minutes.
- Add chopped parsley during the last 15 minutes of cooking.
- Serve over pasta such as penne or fettuccine.

115. Tomato And Chicken Pesto Pasta Recipe

Serving: 6 | Prep: | Cook: 20mins |Ready in:

Ingredients

- 1 lb pre-cooked chicken breast, diced
- 1 lb penne pasta
- 14oz can of diced tomatoes with herbs
- 28oz tomato juice, low sodium
- 1 medium onion, diced
- 2 tbs no-salt italian seasoning
- 4 tbs parmesan cheese, grated
- 2 tbs basil pesto
- 4 tbs 5% cream (you can use 10% cream also)
- salt and pepper to taste

Direction

- In a large pot mix the tomatoes, juice, Italian Seasoning, onion, and pasta.
- Bring to a gentle simmer and stir occasionally to keep the pasta from sticking to the bottom of the pot. (About 15 minutes)
- Mix together the pesto, cream and parmesan cheese and set aside.
- When the pasta is almost done add the diced chicken and adjust the seasoning with salt and pepper to taste.
- When the pasta is al-dente add the pesto mix and stir to combine.
- Take off the heat and allow the pot to "mellow" for about 5 minutes. This should allow it to thicken slightly.
- Serve with additional grated cheese.

116. Tuna And Eggplant Ratatouille(spaghetti Sauce) Over Penne Recipe

Serving: 4 | Prep: | Cook: 25mins |Ready in:

Ingredients

- 3 Tbsp oil
- 1 cup chopped onion
- 2 tsp minced garlic
- 2 cups chopped eggplant (not peeled)
- 1 cup chopped green peppers
- 1 large ripe tomato cubed
- 1 cup tomato juice
- 2 Tbsp tomato paste
- 1 tsp oregano; 1 tsp dried basil; 1/4 tsp black pepper, 1/2 tsp salt
- 1 can tuna, drained
- 1/2 cup chopped fresh parsley
- 1/2 cup parmesan cheese

Direction

- 1. In a large saucepan, heat oil over medium-high heat. Add onions and garlic; cook until softened. Add eggplant and green peppers; cook for 5 minutes or until vegetables are tender and golden. Add tomato paste and sauté for 3 minutes, then add ripe tomatoes, tomatoes juice and the spices, bring to boil. Reduce heat to low; cook covered until tomatoes break down and sauce thickens.
- 2. Add tuna, stirring to break up and turn off the heat.
- 3. Meanwhile, prepare Penne or any kind of Pasta and drain, in a serving bowl, combine pasta, sauce and parsley, toss well. Serve immediately with Parmesan cheese sprinkled on the top.

117. Veggie Pasta Sauce Recipe

Serving: 8 | Prep: | Cook: 60mins |Ready in:

Ingredients

- 2 cans diced tomatoes
- 1 small can tomato paste
- 3 shallots or 1 medium yellow onion, finely chopped
- 1 cup diced white mushrooms

- 1 chopped sweet pepper
- 1/2 cup frozen spinach (or 1 cup fresh)
- 1/2 cup chopped carrots
- 1 diced small zucchini
- 2 tbsp garlic powder
- 2 tbsp basil
- 2 tsp oregano
- dash of ground pepper

Direction

- Combine ingredients in a large pot.
- Simmer on medium low for an hour, or until carrots are soft and the sauce has thickened.

---

118. Vodka Tomato Cream Sauce Recipe

Serving: 4 | Prep: | Cook: 30mins | Ready in:

Ingredients

- 1 tablespoon butter
- 1 tablespoon olive oil
- 1 small chopped onion
- 28 ounces chopped plum tomatoes (I sometimes use tomato puree)
- 1 cup heavy cream
- 1/4 cup vodka
- 1/4 teaspoon crushed red pepper flakes

Direction

- Sauté onion in oil and butter over medium heat.
- Add tomatoes.
- Cook, stirring often for 25 minutes.
- Add cream, vodka and red pepper flakes.
- Simmer until sauce gets to proper consistency, about 2 minutes.

119. Winter Squash Pasta Sauce Recipe

Serving: 2 | Prep: | Cook: 15mins | Ready in:

Ingredients

- 4oz canned pumkin
- 1/3 cup milk
- 1/2 large yellow onion chopped
- 4 cloves garlic
- 1 tablespoon canola oil
- 3/4 cup shredded cheddar cheese
- kosher salt (to taste)
- black pepper (to taste)
- 1 pinch red pepper flakes
- 1/8 teaspoon marjoram
- 1 dash of cinnamon
- cooked pasta shells
- parmesan cheese

Direction

- Heat oil in pan and onion, salt, and pepper. Cook until onion is tender.
- Add sliced garlic and cook until oils are released, about two-three minutes.
- Add pumpkin, milk, red pepper flakes, marjoram, and cinnamon. Stir until well blended and turn to med-low heat and cover for about five minutes.
- Add cheese and mix until melted into sauce.
- Place onto cooked pasta shells and top with parmesan cheese.

120. Zesty Pesto Sauce Recipe

Serving: 46 | Prep: | Cook: | Ready in:

Ingredients

- fresh basil leaves, washed and stemmed, enough to almost fill a standard blender.
- 2 Tablespoons extra-virgin olive oil
- 2 limes or lemons, juiced

- 2 to 5 cloves (or more!) garlic, pressed
- sea salt, to taste
- 1/2 to 1 cup pumpkin seeds, walnuts, [or pine nuts]

Direction

- Grind all ingredients in a blender until you have a course sauce.
- Note: Pesto sauce should never be heated, because this takes away from the freshness of the basil (although it is okay to reheat it along with any leftovers).

---

121.   Raw Tomato Sauce Recipe

Serving: 4 | Prep: | Cook: | Ready in:

Ingredients

- 6 large ripe tomatoes, skinned and chopped
- 1 orange
- 1 lemon
- 4 tbl olive oil
- chopped fresh basil to taste
- sea salt & pepper to taste

Direction

- Place tomatoes in colander
- Grate over both the orange and lemon zest
- Season generously
- Leave to drain for half an hour
- Blitz in a blender with olive oil
- Scatter chopped basil over and you're done

---

122.   Spicy Spaghetti Sauce Recipe

Serving: 24 | Prep: | Cook: 180mins | Ready in:

Ingredients

- 1 -105oz can crushed tomato
- 1 - 14 1/2oz can diced tomato
- 1 - 4oz can tomato paste
- 1/3 cup oliveoil (amber)
- 1 - large green pepper (chopped fine)
- 1 - large onion (chpooed fine)
- 1 Tbsp basil
- 1 Tbsp salt
- 2 Tbsp sugar
- 1 Tbsp corn starch
- 1 tsp oregano
- 1 1/2 tsp cayenne pepper
- 1/2 tsp thyme
- 1/4 cup ramano cheese (finely grated)

Direction

- Using a heavy bottom 8 qt. or larger pot start at the top of the list and assemble the ingredients in the pot.
- Heat slowly to a simmer and simmer for 3 hrs.
- Don't heat too quickly and stir regularly so it doesn't burn to bottom

---

123.   Tomato Sauce Recipe

Serving: 6 | Prep: | Cook: 15mins | Ready in:

Ingredients

- 4 medium tomatoes
- 4-5 shallots
- 2 carrots, diced
- 1 stick celery, chopped finely
- 2 tbsp sun dried tomatoes
- 3 tsp sun dried tomato paste
- 4 fl oz (100ml) white wine
- 4 fl oz (100ml) water
- salt and pepper
- Level tsp sugar
- Handful basil
- Tbsp oil

Direction

- De-skin and deseed the tomatoes and chop roughly.
- Sauté the shallots until golden.
- Add the carrot and celery and cook for 5 minutes.
- Add the tomatoes and cook for a few more minutes, stirring well.
- Add the water, wine and shredded basil and simmer with lid on for 15 minutes.
- Blend.

Index

Conclusion

Thank you again for downloading this book!

I hope you enjoyed reading about my book!

If you enjoyed this book, please take the time to share your thoughts and post a review on Amazon. It'd be greatly appreciated!

Write me an honest review about the book – I truly value your opinion and thoughts and I will incorporate them into my next book, which is already underway.

Thank you!

If you have any questions, **feel free to contact at:** *author@papayarecipes.com*

Lucy Salinas

papayarecipes.com

Printed in Great Britain
by Amazon

14461395R00034